To the Shaws –

In anticipation of a long and
affectionate partnership in the Gospel

Roy Lawson

Very
Sure
of

Religious Language in the Poetry of Robert Browning

E. LeRoy Lawson

1974
Vanderbilt University Press
Nashville, Tennessee

The author and publisher make grateful acknowledgment to the following for permission to quote from the publications listed below:

BOBBS-MERRILL COMPANY, INC. *Naming the Whirlwind: The Renewal of God-Language*, by Langdon Gilkey. Copyright © 1969 by Langdon Gilkey. By permission of the publisher, the Bobbs-Merrill Company, Inc.

CHARLES SCRIBNER'S SONS. *I and Thou*, by Martin Buber, translated by Walter Kaufman. Copyright © 1970 by Charles Scribner's Sons.
The Shaking of the Foundations, by Paul Tillich. Copyright © 1948 by Charles Scribner's Sons. By permission of the publisher.

CORNELL UNIVERSITY PRESS. *The Dialectical Temper: The Rhetorical Art of Robert Browning*, By W. David Shaw. Copyright © 1968 by Cornell University Press. By permission of Cornell University Press.

HARPER AND ROW, PUBLISHERS, INC. *Dynamics of Faith*, by Paul Tillich. Copyright © 1958 by Harper and Row, Publishers, Inc.
The Theology of Hope, by Jürgen Moltmann. Copyright © 1967 by Harper and Row, Publishers, Inc.
How I Believe, by Pierre Teilhard de Chardin, translated by Rene Hague (London: Collins; New York: Harper, 1969), pp. 11-16. English translation copyright © 1969 by William Collins Sons & Co., Ltd. Reprinted by permission.

HARVARD UNIVERSITY PRESS. *Learned Lady: Letters from Robert Browning to Mrs. FitzGerald, 1876-1889*, edited by Edward C. McAleer. Copyright © 1966 by Harvard University Press.

ALEXANDER R. JAMES, *Varieties of Religious Experience*, by William James. Modern Library edition, 1902. Copyright © 1902 by William James. Used by permission of Alexander R. James.

MACMILLAN PUBLISHING COMPANY, INC. *Robert Browning*, by G. K. Chesterton. Copyright ©1951 by the Macmillan Company, New York and London.
The Individual and His Religion, by Gordon W. Allport. Copyright © 1950 by the Macmillan Company, Inc.

JOHN MURRAY, LONDON. *Dearest Isa: Robert Browning's Letters to Isabella Blagden*, edited by Edward C. McAleer. Copyright © 1951 by the University of Texas Press.

OXFORD UNIVERSITY PRESS. *Love, Power and Justice*, by Paul Tillich. Copyright © 1960 by Oxford University Press.

YALE UNIVERSITY PRESS. *Browning's Parleyings: The Autobiography of a Mind*, by William Clyde DeVane. Copyright © 1927 by Yale University Press.
Browning's Characters: A Study in Poetic Technique, by Park Honan. Copyright © 1961 by Yale University Press.
Becoming: Basic Considerations for a Psychology of Personality, by Gordon Allport. Copyright © 1960, by Yale University Press.
Letters of Robert Browning Collected by Thomas J. Wise, by Robert Browning, edited with an Introduction and Notes by Thurman L. Hood. Published in 1933 by Yale University Press. Copyright © 1933 by Thurman L. Hood. By permission of Thurman L. Hood.

YALE REVIEW. "The Private Life of Robert Browning," by Richard D. Altick, in *Yale Review*, XLI, No. 2 (Winter 1952). Copyright © 1951 by Yale University Press.

Library of Congress Cataloguing-in-Publication Data
Lawson, E. Leroy, 1938-
Very Sure of God.

Bibliography: p.
1. Browning, Robert, 1812-1889—Religion and ethics.
I.   Title.
PR4242. R4L3   821'.8   73-21617
ISBN O-8265-1195-3

Acknowledgment

Publication of this book was assisted by
the American Council of Learned Societies
under a grant from
the Andrew W. Mellon Foundation

This book is gratefully dedicated
to my wife, Joy,
and to my children,
Kimberly, Candace, and Lane

Contents

Preface

THIS book is the result of a dialogue between a twentieth-century believer, whose culture has proclaimed God dead, and a nineteenth-century poet whose intellectual milieu was just beginning to call all orthodox belief in God into doubt. A modern believer, accustomed to defending himself and his religion against charges of anti-intellectualism, cowardice, irrelevancy, superstition, or dishonesty, can listen only with sympathy—although not always with approval—to Robert Browning and his several monologuists as they defend their beliefs against similar charges. They are aware of their peculiarities and the hostility or indifference of their auditors. They are dominated by a passion to justify themselves. The modernity of their skeptical faith and the pertinence of their arguments hold Browning's readers in apt attention, forcing some kind of response to their persuasive apologies. As a result, in this study I have had to ask not only what Browning and his speakers believe, but how I feel about what they believe. Browning would not let me remain neutral. Dialogue followed reading, as I questioned Browning's every assertion, frequently challenging his presuppositions and denying his conclusions, often squirming as I recognized myself and my times in his religious poems.

If my discussion of Browning's religion seems to depend unduly heavily upon twentieth-century religious thinkers, it is because Browning's views seem so compatible with them. In several respects he shares their approach to religious questions and their understanding of God-language. Although he differs substantially from Paul Tillich or Jürgen Moltmann or Harvey Cox, to mention but a few modern theologians, Browning's approach to religious questions places him more comfortably in their company than among all but a few theologians of the nineteenth century. These twentieth-century writers are not only theologians, but are students of God who have prepared themselves for theology through advanced studies in related disciplines. The God-question is not metaphysical for them; it is ontological, psychological, linguistic, sociological, and historical. Like Browning, they do not recognize arbitrary distinctions among academic disciplines; they approach God as whole men, seeking to understand Him through the use of every resource—intellectual, emotional, social. As a result of this similarity of approach, Browning's supposedly profound and impenetrable faith yields itself readily to our understanding when studied from a background of reading in these twentieth-century thinkers.

Thanks to this background, we now have new ways to ask, "When Browning says *God,* what does he mean?" In addition to this central question, I have read Browning's poems and letters to find answers to several other key problems about Browning's faith: To what extent was he orthodox in his belief in God and his employment of theological terms? Can one find any real change or development in his personal religious convictions? Does the great Victorian "religious and philosophical teacher" have anything to say about religion to today's somewhat disenchanted audience? Fundamental to this entire study, of course, has been my chief concern: How can an understanding of Browning's personal faith assist his readers to read his religious monologues more sympathetically?

The method employed to answer these questions was as simple as the questions: a word-study of Browning's use of the word *God.* Having first read all of Browning's poems, I then reread them with special attention to every line which mentions God, noting frequency of use, context, usual and unusual connotations, motive and personality of the speaker, and any incidental information offered by the poem. Browning's letters were then compared with his poems, and his early works with his later ones. From these individual and comparative studies, Browning's characteristic uses of the word *God* and the qualities of his personal faith emerged. I then checked my reading of Browning against that of his major critics, and reviewed nineteenth- and twentieth-century theology (to the best of my limited ability in this field). The results confirmed my hypothesis that Browning's faith can be more clearly understood now than at any time since he began writing religious poetry. It is now clear that simplicity and economy rather than complexity characterize his faith. In his disregard for institutions or traditions, his suspicion of language, his epistemological skepticism, and his reliance upon human integrity, he is a spiritual comrade of today's leading religious thinkers.

My debt to Browning scholars is evident throughout the notes. One debt remains to be paid. At the risk of sounding either perfunctory or obsequious, I must thank my advisor, Professor Edgar Hill Duncan of Vanderbilt University, who suggested this project to me. Dr. Duncan possesses a special genius for teaching and for living, in both of which I hope to emulate him.

Very Sure of God

The Return to Respectability

Sun-treader, I believe in God and truth
And Love . . .[1]

Yet the millions have their portion, live their calm
                    or troublous day,
Find significance in fireworks: so, by help of mine,
                    they may
Confidently lay to heart and lock in head their life
                    long—this:
"He there with the brand flamboyant, broad o'er night's
                    forlorn abyss,
Crowned by prose and verse; and wielding, with Wit's
                    bauble, Learning's rod . . .
Well? Why, he at least believed in Soul, was very sure
                    of God."[2]

Nothing about Robert Browning could seem more straightforward and unequivocal than his professions of faith. From his first published poem, the autobiographical *Pauline,* to the equally personal *La Saisiaz,* written forty-five years later—and on to the end of his long and productive career, Browning frequently proclaims his belief in God. Most of his best-known characters, very human personalities struggling with very human problems, are presented as persons who dwell in a world made and dominated by God. This ambience of God seems

1. *Pauline, ll. 1020*–1021. All quotations of Browning's poetry are from *The Works of Robert Browning,* edited by F. G. Kenyon, 10 volumes.
2. *La Saisiaz,* ll. 599–604.

to testify to a devout Christian poet's preoccupation with religion, even in poems whose subjects are secular. In an unstable world, Browning seems to assert, where knowledge is fleeting and deceptive, that at the very least he can be sure of his own existence and of God's:

> I have questioned and am answered. Question, answer
> presuppose
> Two points: that the thing itself which questions,
> answers,—*is*, it knows;
> As it also knows the thing perceived outside itself,
> —a force
> Actual ere its own beginning, operative through its
> course,
> Unaffected by its end,—that this thing likewise needs
> must be;
> Call this—God, then, call that—soul, and both—the
> only facts for me.[3]

Yet in spite of the apparent clarity of these and countless other lines, one of the largest unanswered critical questions in Browning scholarship remains: What did Robert Browning really believe about God?

The question is germane today for several reasons. The first is simply that Browning, whose stature as a poet suffered its share of our century's abusive rejection of all things Victorian, is regaining some of his former respectability. He is no longer just a "typical Victorian," with all the deficiencies that that pejorative term is supposed to imply. He is now being acknowledged, as Ezra Pound called him in 1928, an important progenitor of modern poetry. As Pound is the father of so much in modern poetry, so Browning—especially in his prosody—led the way for Pound and Eliot, among others. Studies of Browning's technique in the light of twentieth-century developments have uncovered his original virtuosity in meter and rhyme. Other studies have examined his dramatic and psychological ability. As a prosodist and dramatic poet, Browning has returned to respectability. Yet our knowledge of Browning remains incomplete until we can account for those fundamental beliefs which undergird his poetry. Is it possible that so original a poet could be only a pedestrian thinker in religious matters? His renewed stature as a poet demands a new critical look at the relationship between his faith and his poetry.

3. *Ibid.,* 216–222.

Another reason for studying Browning's faith is that in many respects he was a Victorian writer, and Victorian England is a subject of growing fascination for our times, thanks to the new perspective from which our century has begun to view that period. Blinded for decades by a belief that modern man had come of age, had outgrown the nineteenth century, the twentieth century has smugly dissociated itself from the religious hypocrisy and conformity it attributed to the Victorians, unwilling to see that morally, religiously, and practically, we are the sons of our Victorian fathers. Now that several decades separate us from them, we have learned to accept—and even appreciate—our fathers' eccentricities. We even admit a few resemblances. The nineteenth century is no longer dismissed with clever witticisms or with the absolutes of adolescent rebellion so characteristic of the 1920s and 1930s. Neither Browning nor his age seems so remote to us as both did in this century's youth, especially in religious questions. Thus Browning scholars now take an interest in his relation to the turbulent religious scene of his time, torn as it was in the cross-currents of controversies which have not yet been resolved. Browning's *Christmas-Eve and Easter-Day, Caliban upon Setebos,* and *Death in a Desert,* to name but a few poems, are studied not only for their poetry but for their contributions to these religious debates. Although never more than a lay theologian, the poet nonetheless spoke to and on behalf of the bewildered believers who were grasping their faith against the attacks of infidels. To study Browning is to learn something of the threat Christian England felt in the writings of the higher critics (David Friedrich Strauss, Ernst Renan, Bishop Colenso, the *Essays and Reviews* writers). The threat is reflected in his poems, as are the English hostility toward the foreign ostentations of Roman Catholicism and the Christian clergy's sweeping condemnations of the atheism believed to adhere to the new theories of evolution, both Darwinian and Spencerian. Browning defended his personal Christianity against these challengers. As a result, his polemical poems expose both the current religious trends and the basis of his own faith.

To twentieth-century critics, Browning is a progressive innovator in prosody and, in his dramatic monologues, an inventor of characters worthy of comparison with Shakespeare. But as a religious thinker, he has remained hopelessly Victorian or even pre-Victorian. Although aware of the severe intellectual challenges to Christianity, Browning's apparent optimism has impressed these critics as vacuous and insincere. His return to respectability has not included religious respectability. In view of the tensions of his times, when thinking men felt all traditional values and certainties crumbling beneath their feet, when God seemed more and more remote and a new godless determinism more and more assured, they asked how an unusually well-informed person like Browning could assert so confidently, "I believe in God." Their question echoes Thomas Hardy's: "The longer I live the more does Browning's character seem the literary puzzle of the nineteenth century. How could smug Christian optimism worthy of a dissenting grocer find a place inside a man who was so vast a seer and feeler when on neutral ground?"[4] How *did* Browning reconcile the new science and the old faith? What did the term *God* mean to him?

Browning's critics raise these questions urgently. If we are sons of our Victorian fathers, and if the questions have any meaning for Browning, then they are essential in our century. What can God mean today, in a society so closely linked to Browning's own? Implicit in these questions is the paradox of both the nineteenth and twentieth centuries: In spite of the relentless trends toward "secularism," "scientism," "psychologism," and "individualism," there is no indication that either interest in God or the use of God-language has diminished. Browning's preoccupation with religious questions seems equally symbolic of his time and ours.

Victorian England witnessed the relentless advance of secularization with its accompanying complications. The period gave birth to astounding innovations in communication, technology, and industry. But it also gave birth to diverse and intense religious movements which seem to contradict the apparent secularism of the time: the Salvation Army, The Oxford Movement, the Evangelical Revival, Christian Science. Our own century, with its aluminum and steel monuments to our technological and scientific virtuosity, has paradoxically encouraged many of the above movements and generated many of its own, including such bizarre forms as devil worship and astrology. The fact that religious interest does not diminish even in this thoroughly "scientific" day makes a study of Browning's faith no mere academic inquiry into a historical phenomenon. An inquiry into the nature of Browning's belief becomes a study of the nature of belief itself. Unable to dismiss religion as simply the superstitions of pre-scientific man or the haven of refuge for socially inept persons, contem-

---

4. Thomas Hardy to Edmund Gosse. Quoted in Boyd Litzinger, *Time's Revenges: Browning's Reputation as a Thinker, 1889–1962*, p. 16.

porary students of human behavior must account for the persistence of belief in God. Browning's reliance upon God-language and his fascination with religious issues no longer seem quite so foreign as they did only a few decades ago. He is one of us.

These comments should not imply a desire to return to the Victorian and Edwardian view of Browning as a great religious and philosophical teacher. Our generation will read Browning as a poet, not as a prophet. He will no longer be subjected to the adulation or condemnation which he so long endured from those who read him more for his spiritual message than for his poetry. His reputation has not yet fully recovered from these judgments upon him.

To understand Browning's current reputation as a thinker, it is necessary to review the praise and abuse followers and critics have heaped upon him through the decades. After enduring near-obscurity for more than twenty years (from the publication of *Sordello*—a calamity for his literary reputation—in 1840 to that of *Dramatis Personae* in 1864), he began his steady climb to fame which lasted into the third decade of the twentieth century. The *Athenaeum* set the tone for the kind of favorable commentary to come when it hailed the 1868–1869 publication of *The Ring and the Book* as "the most precious and profound spiritual treasure that England has produced since the days of Shakespeare."[5] Of course, there were less favorable reviews; but from the appearance of *The Ring and the Book,* Browning enjoyed an adoring audience of disciples who read him more eagerly for his spiritual insights than for his poetry.

Typical of Browning's admirers was Dr. Edward Berdoe, author of *Browning and the Christian Faith.* A professed agnostic whose many years of reading had led him to reject the claims of Christianity because of the insufficiency of scientific evidence to support them, he one day heard Mr. Moncure Conway lecture on Browning's *Sordello.* Impressed, he bought a complete set of Browning's poems and read them eagerly, beginning with *Saul,* then *Paracelsus, Men and Women,* and *A Death in the Desert.* Through these works he found answers to all his questions and he acknowledged Browning as the religious teacher he needed. He joined the London Browning Society as others join a church, and devoted himself to propagating his new-found gospel.

Others found similar help. Such enthusiasm seldom remains private. The Browning Society, founded by Miss Hickey and F. J. Furnivall

5. *Athenaeum,* No. 2160, March 20, 1869.

in 1881, provided a forum for public exposition of his poems for their spiritual meanings, with elaborate commentaries written on single lines and images, as well as on entire poems. Browning's popularity can be measured by the growth of the societies. By 1884 there were at least twenty-two (including several in Chicago and one in Melbourne), and by the time of Browning's death, practically every major metropolis could boast its own society. Browning the poet had been apotheosized: he was Browning the Prophet, the Seer, the Oracle, the Philosopher. His readers were not students; they were disciples. But the societies were not the assemblies of single-minded and simple-minded disciples such as this statement—or the delightful caricature by Max Beerbohm—might suggest. (Beerbohm's sketch presents an elegantly attired silver-maned-and-bearded Browning stirring his tea, seated in the center of a circle of emaciated, bald, and bespectacled men and pious, plain, and singularly unattractive women.) To mention that George Bernard Shaw was an early member is to dispel any notions of unanimity of judgment. Heresies abounded. Most of the papers, however, support later criticisms of the societies for being too eager to worship Browning for his complex spiritual wisdom. By and large, Browningites looked to Browning to defend them and their faith against their enemies: evolution, liberalism, secularism, individualism. They wanted to believe what they thought he believed. The poetry was lost in the philosophy.

It is not surprising, then, that two eminent philosophers should attempt to correct what was, to them, the obvious injustice done by the societies and other devotees. The success of Henry Jones and George Santayana and the general fair balance of their judgments against Browning the philosopher are still apparent today; no Browning student can avoid considering and answering their charges. As a result, all subsequent criticism of Browning's religious thought has sought either to corroborate, modify, or refute them.

Jones published *Browning as a Philosophical and Religious Teacher* in 1891, a little more than a year after the poet's death. Placing Browning among the philosophers—a place which Browning himself did not claim—he praised the poet as an earnest and systematic teacher of idealism. Having "elevated" Browning to his own philosophical fraternity, Jones then attacked the inconsistencies within his system, finding the source of his philosophical difficulties in his simultaneous adoption of a theory of the failure of knowledge and a belief in the moral progress of man. He charges Browning with forcing a severance between the head and the heart, the intellect and the emotions, a severance which should lead logically to agnoticism about God and pessimism about man. Jones is astonished to find Browning ignoring the consequences of his epistemology and defending human ignorance of God's will as essential to moral growth. Jones is perhaps too thoroughly systematic to deal comprehensively with one less systematic, upon whom he imposes his own zeal for systematic order. Ignoring not only the poet's peculiar tools and techniques but also all nonphilosophical religious considerations which were so important to Browning (biblical Christianity, love between human beings, importance of existential choice, the impact of higher criticism—and many other subjects), Jones concentrates solely upon the elements of idealistic philosophy in Browning's poetry, thus missing the poetic and polemic characteristics. He peremptorily condemns Browning's lack of a philosophical system, demanding what the poet is not prepared to give. In attempting a corrective to the Browning Society excesses, Jones inadvertently stumbles into their fellowship by treating Browning so exclusively as a philosopher. So convincingly does Jones write, however, that no concerted effort was made to refute his charges that Browning severed feeling from intelligence (in order to be able to ignore intellectual arguments when they countered his emotional optimism) until the 1960s, in the work of Philip Drew and Norton Crowell. Drew stresses the tentativeness of Browning's questions and the unprejudiced openmindedness of his search for answers;[6] Crowell sees Browning's philosophical beliefs as unified and dovetailed rather than fragmented.[7]

The second major attack upon Browning was even more devastating. "The Poetry of Barbarism," by George Santayana, first appeared in *Interpretations of Poetry and Religion* in 1900. The stature of the critic, the energy of his attack, the more inclusive treatment of the poetry as well the philosophy, and the brilliance of the writing guaranteed a respectful hearing for its author. Santayana couples Browning with Whitman as examples of modern poets who "are things of shreds and patches; they give us episodes and studies, a sketch on this curiosity, a glimpse of that romance; they have no total vision, no grasp of the whole reality, and consequently no capacity for a sane and steady idealization." In reading Browning, "we are in the presence of a barbaric genius, of a truncated imagination, of a thought and

6. "Henry Jones on Browning's Optimism," pp. 29–41.

7. *The Triple Soul: Browning's Theory of Knowledge,* and *The Convex Glass: The Mind of Robert Browning.*

an art inchoate and ill-digested, of a volcanic eruption that tosses itself quite blindly and ineffectually into the sky."[8] Santayana's complaint with Browning differs diametrically from Jones's. Whereas Jones faulted the poet for having an inconsistent idealism, Santayana can find no idealism in him at all. Not ideas, but things are the stuff of Browning's poetry. Not ideals, but temperament is at the core of Browning's religion: Santayana finds Browning's religion to have more in common with the worship of Thor or Odin than of Christ. This, says Santayana, is the religion of the "poetry of barbarism."

Santayana's words, written in 1900, and Jones's earlier work remained the minority report for the next two decades. Browning was still riding the crest of his popularity, so the iconoclastic impact of Jones's and Santayana's essays had to await the more general reaction to "Victorianism." In the early 1900s, most writers on Browning still eulogized him as the great spiritual leader.[9] Browning was "the poet who has given the world the utmost certainty of God, the soul and immortality, and the most inspiring ideals of human love.[10] His poetry contains "a message of Life, of Hope, of Spiritual Realities . . . a message that shall irradiate life, give courage to the faint-hearted, and sustain with a vision of glorious hope all storm-tossed, tried and tempted souls."[11] As recently as 1962, one author could still say, "There is, indeed, no other great English poet so consistently and constantly Christian as Browning."[12]

These words do not represent Browning's reputation at midcentury, however. Following the flourish of Browning studies during his centennial decade (1910s), when he received enthusiastically sympathetic treatment, Browning's reputation as a religious thinker went into the eclipse from which it has not yet emerged. His famed optimism, which his Victorian contemporaries found so helpful, sounded hollow and insincere to post-World War and depression audiences. There was little in their world to confirm what they were told was Browning's fundamental belief: "God's in his heaven, / All's

8. "The Poetry of Barbarism," reprinted in *Robert Browning*, p. 18.

9. This review of Browning's reception as a religious thinker is necessarily incomplete. See also Boyd Litzinger, *Time's Revenges;* F. R. G. Duckworth, *Browning: Background and conflict;* Frederic E. Faverty, *The Victorian Poets: A Guide to Research*, second ed.; Boyd Litzinger and K. L. Knickerbocker, editors, *The Browning Critics*.

10. Helen A. Clarke, *Browning and His Century*, p. 370.

11. Litzinger, p. 51.

12. Dallas Kenmare, *An End to Darkness: A New Approach to Robert Browning and His Work*, p. 191.

right with the world."[13] A new note of irritation began to be heard in Browning criticism. Critics commenced to categorize more specifically the exact nature of his faith or to find some psychological explanation for what by now had begun to appear empty enthusiasm. To a war-torn and poverty-haunted people, many of Browning's poems sounded like the pious platitudes of a well-fed, comfortable clergyman.

Those who continued to admire Browning as a religious teacher sought other grounds than philosophical idealism or doctrinal consistency as the source of his strength. The most persistent label attached to him, and perhaps the least appropriate of all, was *mystic*. As early as 1905, Dean Inge devoted thirty-two pages of his *Studies of English Mystics* to Browning.[14] By employing an unusually inclusive definition of *mystic*, he can so categorize Browning because of "his profound belief in a perfect spiritual world, in which all broken fragments are made whole, all riddles solved, all legitimate hopes satisfied." Rufus Jones, writing in 1923, also calls Browning a mystic, "a person who had first-hand experiences of God and could say with his John in the desert, 'I saw.'"[15] These efforts, however, evidence the decline of Browning's stature from the late Victorian days, when he was revered as almost without peer. Then such attempts to place him among others would have been blasphemy. He now quietly takes his place among the seers, the nonrationalists, and intuitive apprehenders of spiritual experience. But to a civilization moving steadily toward even greater secularization, with its accompanying anonymity and isolation, such mystical explanations seemed inadequate at best, and the spiritual pilgrims seeking Browning's oracular wisdom became fewer with each passing year.

As his personal authority diminished, Browning's critics—those who cared enough to write about him in the second quarter of this century—grew emboldened. Unawed by his supposed profundity, impatient with his apparent contradictions, and dismayed by what seemed to be intellectual cowardice, they moved him from the pulpit to the laboratory where, analyzing him under microscope and upon couch, they pronounced him dead as a spiritual leader. They then performed an autopsy to find the cause of his failure. Stewart W. Holmes exemplifies these technicians.[16] Studying *Sordello* with Jungian

13. *Pippa Passes*, I, 227–228.
14. William Ralph Inge, pp. 207–239.
15. "Mysticism in Robert Browning," *The Biblical Review* VIII, 232–233.
16. "Browning: Semantic Stutter," *Publication of the Modern Language Association* LX (1946), 255. See also his "Browning's *Sordello* and Jung," *PMLA* XVI (1941), 758–796.

psychotherapeutic theories, he found in Browning an "internal confusion" which the poet attempted to express (for the last time in *Sordello*) but at which attempts he failed. Hence, from *Sordello* on, Browning eschewed analytical writing and personal revelation, hiding himself in the more objective, dramatic monologues. His internal confusion and his inability to articulate with more than "semantic stutterings" prevented his speaking effectively in the first person about life's deepest questions. Another explanation was offered in 1952 by Richard Altick, who published an equally damning article on Browning's private life. If anyone could still trust Browning as a religious teacher after reading Altick, his faith was immovable indeed. Altick was convinced that the poet's famous good health and robust vigor covered an unhealthy, insecure, unreliable personality:

> His "healthiness" seems actually unhealthy; a feverish
> flush on the cheeks, a fantastic cheerfulness of view, a
> serious malady within. We can grant to any poet a normal
> degree of satisfaction with the smooth flow of his
> endocrines, but in Browning's poetry there persists
> a palpable excess of health.[17]

Such insalubrious healthiness, insists Altick, is not to be trusted: "His fervent celebration of the glories of the incomplete, the imperfect, as being part of God's inscrutable but unquestionable plan for men, is far less the manifestation of an intellectual conviction than it is the result of Browning's growing need to salve his awareness of the future."[18] This same theme is echoed by Hoxie Fairchild in his massive study of religion in English literature. He finds "something insecure about the man's personality, something not quite sound or genuine." Using the same argument as Altick's, "the poet doth protest too much," he argues that "no one who is really strong and confident makes so much noise about it. His robustious poetry contrasts embarrassingly with his sedentary, unadventurous, nineteenth-century-bourgeois life."[19] Betty Miller's persuasive biography of Browning opens with an emphasis upon his hypochondria to establish the tone for another—and this one a most seductive—psychological analysis of a poet whose perverted affection for his mother warped his emotional

---

17. Richard D. Altick, "The Private Life of Robert Browning," *Yale Review* XLI (December 1951). Reprinted in *The Browning Critics*, p. 249.
18. *Ibid.*, p. 253.
19. *Religious Trends in English Poetry*, vol. IV: *1830–1880*, p. 135.

ufe throughout maturity as well as in his sheltered and pampered childhood. Mrs. Miller paints a picture of a self-centered and self-indulgent boy, satisfied in every neurotic whim, to that of the grown mama's boy, dependent upon his parents until his marriage, then upon his wife, a mother-substitute six years his senior. Mrs. Miller gives us an insecure, dependent personality whose opinions on the weather, no less than about God, must be questioned.

A reaction to such subjective psychological analyses has now come about. In the past fifteen years, scholars have dealt much less impressionistically with Browning. As a result, Browning scholarship is better than it has ever been. A few studies deserve special praise. Robert Langbaum's excellent *Poetry of Experience,* a study of the dramatic monologue, is the definitive study of both the subjective and the objective criteria of the genre. E. D. H. Johnson's *Alien Vision of Victorian Poetry* releases Browning from his bondage to Victorian intellectual and spiritual conventions and sets him in opposition to the cliches of his day. It is an important first step in the study of Browning's faith. J. Hillis Miller's provocative *Disappearance of God* is the most suggestive introduction to the poet's religious convictions to date, seeing the heart of Browning as "a struggle of irreconcilable forces," in a world which has experienced the "withdrawal of God and the consequent impoverishment of man and his surroundings."[20] Several other recent authors have reasserted the unity of Browning's vision in response to those critics who have followed Jones in criticizing Browning for severing thought from feeling. Thus, after several decades of somnolence, Browning criticism is awakening to the challenges of both the creative poet and the unorthodox thinker.

The history of literary criticism has been defined as "largely the history of the changing questions we ask about works of art."[21] It could also be called asking the same old questions in new ways. The vital issues with which all the arts have always concerned themselves have not really changed, but the vocabulary we employ in talking about those issues has. Thus each generation reads the masterpieces of the past as they have never been read before, aided by new semantic tools which illuminate obscure passages which awaited time's unfolding revelation. Our century has developed such conceptual tools for analyzing language. When applied to religious language, they enable

20. Page 99.
21. Robert Langbaum, "Browning and the Question of Myth," *PMLA* LXXXI (1966), 575.

us to ask the old questions in ways unknown to Browning's Victorian and Edwardian readers, and to receive new answers. Robert Langbaum undoubtedly has these linguistic and philosophical developments in mind when he writes that Browning was telling his age that "they were asking the wrong questions of the universe; and that he was himself reaching toward the sort of questions for which the proper vocabulary has been supplied only in our time through the philosophies of existentialism and symbolic form."[22] The requisite vocabulary is now available, as Langbaum suggests, not only in the philosophies of existentialism and symbolic form, but also in other fields. Psychology, for example, dominated for so long by Freudian terminology (which appears to be singularly incapable of accounting for Browning's "normal" behavior) has begun to reject the narrow determinism of Freud for a more flexible goal-oriented explanation of man's behavior.

Theology, the specific interest of this book, has re-examined its concepts in defending itself from the spectacular attacks of the radical theologians of the 1960s, who popularized Nietzsche's famous cry, "God is dead," and has offered some rather convincing proof that God is really not so dead, after all. Their work contributes invaluable aids for a study of Browning's use of religious language. It is inevitable that interest in Browning's religious thought should now be revived at precisely the time when theologians are successfully refuting the charge that God is dead. As the theologians have found their defense in the nature of God-language itself, so Browning critics have been forced to study Browning's use of religious language. That study could not have been undertaken in Browning's time—in fact, it could scarcely have been made prior to the battle over God-language which was waged in the 1960s, because Browning's religious language has many more affinities with that of our time than with any decade prior to the sixties.

These twentieth-century concepts can be adopted, however, only after surveying Browning's religious milieu, placing it in the context of Christianity's larger history. The Victorian period had already begun to feel the turbulence of change which futurists predict will continue to accelerate. The Victorians, like ourselves, were convinced that they were living in an age of transition. This consciousness of change pervaded every aspect of Victorian life: industrial growth and development, social mobility, scientific discovery, philosophical

22. Review of Boyd Litzinger's *Time's Revenges* in *Victorian Poetry* III, 148.

and intellectual advancement, and moral and religious restlessness. In an age which feels itself losing its grip on the traditional and groping hesitantly into the unknown, apathy about basic human concerns is impossible. All positions are supported with gusto. The Victorian zeal did not necessarily rise out of their confidence, at least in religion and philosophy. If it was an age of faith, it was even more an age of doubt.

At least three broadly defined positions were staked out in the ecclesiastical world, and they were rigorously defended. The first was conservative Protestantism, including the various dissenting and independent groups and a majority of the Anglicans. Although these groups differed considerably in church polity and ritual, they were similar in finding the ultimate authority for personal and church life in the Holy Scriptures, which they viewed as the infallible Word of God. Insulated from their more liberal contemporaries on the Continent until the 1860s, they were not forced to confront the challenges, already present in Continental theology, which would divide them after 1860. This evangelical protestantism, accepting scriptural doctrines concerning God and man (either formalized in the Thirty-Nine Articles or informally reiterated in dissenting chapels), stressed God's omnipotence and man's worthlessness before him.

In the general spirit of reform that accompanied the passage of the Reform Bill of 1832, this prevailing evangelical temper fell under attack from two opposite quarters. John Keble's sermon on National Apostacy in 1833 began the Oxford Movement. Members of this effort did not concentrate their energies upon the individual salvation stressed by conservative Christianity; rather, they reasserted the role of the Church, stressing its authority, its sacerdotal responsibilities, and its distinction from what Morley had called "the House of Commons' view of human life."[23] They propagated their views primarily through a series of *Tracts* published between September 9, 1833, and January 25, 1841, with John Henry Newman early emerging as the foremost polemicist of the group. The radical insistence upon the divine authority of the church and its clergy, and the impartial analyses of the precarious position of the Anglican church as the *via media* between Roman Catholicism and dissent (as evidenced so blatantly in Newman's famous *Tract 90*, "Remarks on certain passages in the Thirty-nine Articles," January 25, 1841), finally led Newman from the Anglican fold into the Roman Catholic Church. The defection of so prominent

23. *On Compromise*, p. 95. Quoted in Buckley, p. 119.

a clergyman and several of his followers into the foreign church unsettled the conservative establishment, especially as Roman Catholicism later grew into a major religious force in England.

The more insidious and powerful threat to evangelical Christianity came from another direction: rationalistic liberalism. For our purposes, this is the most important aspect of the nineteenth-century religious scene, because it is here—if anywhere—rather than in the evangelicism of his youth, that the mature Browning belongs, even though he fought several of its leaders in his poems and differed substantially from some of their premises, retaining several evangelical convictions. Conservative Protestant Christianity rests its case ultimately on the authority of the divinely inspired Holy Scriptures, and Roman Catholicism rests its case on the authority of the divinely ordained Church. Contrary to both of them, liberal Christianity finds it impossible to release individual human responsibility to any external authority. While still respecting the scriptures as the traditional source of cultural values and myths, it subjects them to personal reason and feeling. Conservative theology deduces its doctrines from tradition, biblical or ecclesiastical. Liberal theology induces its creeds from the evidence of experience. Undoubtedly, even in the heart of the medieval Age of Faith, most men reserved the right of final judgment for themselves. But never before the nineteenth century did church leaders defend such liberalism as Christianity. From the turning point in the shift of theology from deduction to induction, generally conceded to be Friederich Schleiermacher's 1799 publication *On Religion: Addresses in Response to Its Cultured Critics*,[24] theology has not been able to content itself with exposition of its doctrines and polemics against heresy. Instead, its business has become defense and interpretation of itself to a secular audience, a defense characterized more by accommodation than separation. In agreeing to meet its critics on their grounds, theology relinquished its time-honored right to appeal to the Scriptures, the Fathers, and ecclesiastical practice as acceptable authorities. It had to find a new vocabulary for itself, adopting cultural and relative terms into which to translate the rigid formulae of its creeds and articles. No longer could it demand that human reason bow before the unquestioned infallibility of the depository of faith. Nothing was any longer sacred just because it was religious.

---

24. Translated by Terence N. Tice. Another title, *On Religion; Speeches to Its Cultured Despisers,* translated by John Oman, more clearly indicates the newly defensive position of Christian theology.

In England, the full impact of this new challenge to the conservative position was felt first in the 1860s. Some prior studies had caused slight ripples, but the waves of controversy which permanently changed English theology did not arrive until then. In Old Testament studies, the major crisis came with Bishop Colenso's *Pentateuch and Joshua Critically Examined.* Appearing in 1862, its readers' response was swift and frightened. The bishop, a former missionary to Natal who was also a competent mathematician, could not accept the errors he found in the figures in the Pentateuch. He submitted the first six books of the Old Testament to a critical scrutiny that its holy nature had always hitherto been able to prevent, and horrified his readers with his objective treatment. Undoubtedly his position as a bishop in the church added to their discomfort. The English reading public had been shocked just two years earlier when *Essays and Reviews* was published by seven authors, six of whom were Church of England divines. Attempting to introduce German higher criticism into England, they called for honest inquiry into the Scriptures in light of scientific discoveries and methodology. The seven writers agreed to accept the truth at all costs, even if the result would be loss of faith in the Scriptures. A righteous indignation protested against such heresy. The writers were denounced as "Septem Contra Christum." In the company of Colenso's study of the Old Testament and recent New Testament studies, *Essays and Reviews* rapidly established itself as one of the primary documents of the liberal movement.

New Testament studies also reached their greatest impact in the 1860s, but the ground had been well cultivated by the German higher critic David Frederick Strauss. In 1835, Strauss published *Das Leben Jesu,* the pioneer work of New Testament higher criticism. Reading the Scriptures with the tools of scientific analysis and the presuppositions of rationalistic empiricism, Strauss sought to replace blind trust in infallible inspiration with a new objective but truthful account of Jesus. Miracles were given naturalistic explanations, supernatural events were accounted for as myths—which, though necessary for religious expression, nonetheless are myths. Strauss stripped Jesus' biography of these multiplied myths attached to him. This demythologized biography of Christ arrived in England in George Eliot's 1846 translation of it and attracted scholarly interest. In 1863, Ernst Renan published his *La Vie de Jesus,* a novelistic biography which built on Strauss's work, reading the scriptures in the same rationalistic manner that Strauss employed, but concentrating on Jesus' personality rather than demythologizing the history of his life. Reaction to Renan

17

could only believe in, but not prove God. Romantic philosophies concerned themselves with the presence of imminence of the absolute. God is not the totally separate Other, but the All-Pervasive. In the later half of the nineteenth century, evolutionistic and process forms led to the disappearance of absolutes entirely, to be replaced by process, flux, change. The consciousness of a transcendent order has shifted from the rationally apprehensible and explicable to a felt or sensed order, incapable of proof or demonstration. What was God to the Enlightened thinker was not God to the Romantic or his successors.

In his transitional world, with its sense of being always on the way, the nineteenth-century liberal could not justify a belief in truth "once for all delivered" either to an institution (church) or a body of literature (Bible). Being, as a descendant of Kantian skepticism and British "common sense," unable philosophically to prove or disprove God's existence, he trusted in his rational or intuitive powers alone. While fundamentalist evangelical Christians still spoke passionately about a personal or metaphysical God, liberal Christians scoffed at such superstition. Gone were the old absolutes; gone was the ordered universe. But at least man remained, the pinnacle of creation (or evolution, depending on one's theory of origins), endowed with almost immeasurable rational and intuitive powers.

Most late nineteenth-century liberals trusted their rational rather than their intuitive powers in religious matters. Theirs was a rationalism reminiscent of eighteenth-century Deism and prophetic of early twentieth-century theological liberalism in its acceptance of human intelligence as final arbiter in religion. Of course, twentieth-century liberal theology could no longer base itself on the eternal, unchanging truths which supported Deism. The intervening philosophical and institutional changes wrought in the nineteenth century permanently destroyed the Deistic universe. But they had not yet, in the first half of our century, destroyed faith in human reason. It is not strange, then, that philosophical and religious students of Browning in this period were somewhat embarrassed by Robert Browning. Jones and Santayana were right: as a systematic, rational philosopher, Browning fails. He fails precisely because he can never totally embrace logic and rationality as final religious authorities. Full understanding of Browning's religious position has had to await theology's rejection of rational liberalism.

That rejection has come. To many serious thinkers, theological rationalism has proved inadequate to account for these irrepressible but irrational religious impulses of man. Further, with the developments in positivism, existentialism, and empirical naturalism, all rationalistic philosophical systems (including those of such giants as Barth, Brunner, Bultmann, and, to an extent, Tillich) have been challenged as ephemeral structures built of airy words, full of erudition and profundity—but signifying nothing. They are built, radical theologians like William Hamilton and Thomas Altizer believe, upon foundations which do not exist. "Death of God" theologians, in fact, have concluded that all God-language upon which rational theological systems have built is valueless. They point to the weakness of human faith and the absence of God from the human experience, the meaninglessness of all metaphysical language, and the impossibility—even the immorality—of interpreting historical evil in any terms but purely secular ones.[27]

We have arrived at the end of the journey which started in the Renaissance. The questioning spirit that arose then, with its assertion of man's magnificent potential and accomplishments, which transferred religious authority from the immovable Church to the more flexible and interpretable Scriptures, and which then, in the nineteenth century, attacked the Scriptures and, by implication, any scriptural assertions, in the twentieth century has questioned and finally denied any meaning to our God-language.

It is no wonder, then, that the religious statements of a poet who unashamedly announces "I believe in God" should be so summarily dismissed by readers who have, since at least 1860, first been taught to place their ultimate faith in rational or naturalistic propositions and then to measure all truth on the severely restrictive scales of empiricism. And when this movement reached its ultimate within the last decade, readers learned that any statements at all about God—either affirming or denying him—are without meaning. Browning's God-language has seemed remote indeed.

But *God* refuses to die. The Death-of-God movement of the sixties has been replaced by new theologies attempting to account for the persistence of God-language. As a result of these new studies in religious language, it is now possible to take Browning's religious professions quite seriously. We can now ask, "But when Browning said *God,* what did he mean?" Without at all suggesting any return to an older theological position, and without denying the cultural flavor of religious language, contemporary writers like Harvey Cox, Bishop Robinson,

27. See Langdon Gilkey, *Naming the Whirlwind: The Renewal of God-Language.*

Langdon Gilkey, Jürgen Moltmann, and Wolfhart Pannenberg (to name but a few) have re-examined such language, firmly denying its meaninglessness to believers. Undoubtedly, the secular spirit of the twentieth century makes any references to God more difficult than in previous centuries; nonetheless, *God* has resisted all efforts to denigrate it. While organized religion has been under severe attack, individual religiosity continues to flourish, at times expressed in somewhat bizarre forms. Evidences of the popularity of what a strict rationalist could only call superstition abound. The positivistic and radical attacks upon religion, which would eliminate superstition and rationalism alike, have failed. Ironically, their failure is precisely that of the systems they have attacked. They have been as militantly rationalistic as the systematizers. They, too, have insufficiently accounted for man's inner longings for religious experience and for some language to express that experience. They have limited language as radically as they have limited religion, claiming that words without objective referents are meaningless.

Religious language, however, is not scientific language. As Langdon Gilkey insists, three indispensable features distinguish religious language from other kinds:

> (1) It is multivalent or doubly intentional, referring both to the finite world and to the sacred and the ultimate that is manifest in and through the finite. (2) It is concerned with existential or ultimate issues of life, the questions that involve us because they center around the security, meanings, frustrations, and hopes of our existence both individual and social. (3) It provides crucial models or norms by which life is directed and judged, and so by which culture as a whole is itself guided and assessed.[28]

It is not, then denotative, and not strictly referential. What is important to Gilkey is to recognize that even though our human reasoning and ability to articulate may be limited and our vocabulary imprecise, ontologically man apprehends dimensions of reality which cry out for expression. Some kind of religious language is thus a psychological and cultural necessity. It may not reveal the nature of God, but it does provide clues to the identity of a believer who calls upon his name.

Thus the recent revival of respect for God-language within the liberal religious tradition acknowledges that, even though man may

28. *Ibid.*, p. 295.

possess reasoning powers, he is not fundamentally rational. He apprehends his world as a total man. There is more to himself and his world than reason alone can know. To his reason and his sense, he must join his intuitive apprehensions. This fact has been slowly gaining a foothold in Western philosophy over the past centuries, accompanying the rise of individualism we have traced, but it gained respectability as a viable philosophical attitude only in our century. Descartes, the "father of modern philosophy" who introduced the overriding preoccupation with epistemology which has motivated rationalistic theologies, was also the father of rationalistic epistemology's supreme challenger, irrationalistic existentialism. When he systematically set himself to doubt everything, he still could conclude *Cogito, ergo sum.* With these words he expressed the essence of contemporary existentialism, a philosophy which posits nothing except "I am." All other states of being must be deduced from this statement of faith in one's own existence. Presuppositions such as Locke's *tabula rasa,* or Kant's categories, or the Absolutes of idealism, or the *stimulus-response* of behaviorism are interesting conjectures but invalid generalizations about man, because they are based upon some concept of essence, not individual existence. To say that man is *essentially* anything is to presuppose a commonality among the species which veers dangerously near either determinism or *a priori* thinking. The existentialist, like Descartes, can only say "I am." Living in and influenced by his context, he nonetheless is able to realize a potential not entirely determined by the laws of that context. He is autonomous, free to become.

Stated baldly, existentialism teaches that it is every man for himself. There are no external givens; there is no absolute, immovable, static order or Orderer. There is only the reality of the given moment, the possibility of immediate choice in concrete situations.

Of course, existential arguments have been used throughout religious history. It is possible, for example, to contrast the personal, unphilosophical, passionate Hebrew religion with the more rationalistic and abstract Greek philosophies; by contrast, the Hebrew seems strongly existential. Thus, Abraham, according to Kierkegaard, becomes the archetypal man of faith, obeying God's orders to slay Isaac against all arguments of reason and custom.[29] And Job faces God, "not by the way of reason but by the confrontation of the whole

29. Soren Kierkegaard, *Fear and Trembling and The Sickness unto Death,* translated by Walter Lowrie, pp. 26–132.

man . . . in the fullness and violence of his passion with the unknowable and overwhelming God."[30] Christian church history is also replete with examples of men who acted existentially. The great church father Tertullian, often cited as a precursor of Kierkegaard, defended his faith in the third century with existentialist paradox: "The Son of God was crucified; I am unashamed of it because men must needs be ashamed of it. And the Son of God died; it is by all means to be believed, because it is absurd. And He was buried and rose again; the fact is certain because it is impossible."[31] However, Tertullian's dependence upon the argument from absurdity differs from the existential position of the nineteenth and twentieth centuries. Job or Tertullian could speak about God from within a well-defined religious heritage which accepted fully, although it could not always explain, the existence of God. Faith in their religious traditions, in a possible relationship between God and man, and in the integrity of the human mind—all these had not yet been challenged. But by the nineteenth century, the security of theocentric culture no longer existed. God had disappeared. Only the image of God remained. Since God was no longer central, then the self must become assertive, imposing individual meaning upon the universe from which it once deduced its meaning. Men could still speak freely and meaningfully of a world larger—even infinitely larger—than themselves, but the importance of that world derived from personal human experience.

No summary statement can do justice to the diversity of religious opinions by men commonly called existentialists today. Their philosophies are as singular as their names: Heidigger, Nietzsche, Kierkegaard, Sartre, Camus, Unamuno, Buber, Tillich, Maritain, Berdyaev. Certain generalizations, however, can be suggested with the understanding that the individual authors will vary—or even dissent from—one or another of them. Beginning with the fact that a man exists, uniquely, the existentialist reacts strongly to any attempt to partition him into segments: physical, emotional, or rational. Such terms, if they must be used, are only heuristic conveniences. He is a man experiencing, not just a mind thinking or a heart feeling or nerve-endings sensing. He experiences the concrete, not the abstract. Hence any attempted explanation for his behavior must be rooted in things, places, persons, events.

30. William Barrett, *Irrational Man: A Study in Existential Philosophy*, p. 73. See Barrett for several other examples, including Pascal, Augustine, even St. Thomas.

31. *Ibid.*, pp. 94–95.

To read Browning's poetry after reading twentieth-century existentialist literature is to realize both his kinship to and his separation from it. As a general rule, the "sense of loss, alienation, and despair" of a Sartre, for example, was not the dominant mood of Browning. He did not choose to view the world as absurd or meaningless or without order—but he did share the belief that he must choose for himself how he would view it. In other respects, Browning is at home among the existentialists: he places individual freedom above custom, dynamic growth above abstract order, intuition and experience above—but not divorced from—reason, individual above social man. Much of his religious thought was misinterpreted by almost all his Victorian readers, because Browning's existentialist frame of reference was ahead of them. His persistence in using traditional religious vocabulary to express an existential attitude had to await twentieth-century philosophic and literary developments for full explication. A personal faith stressing the uniqueness and isolation of the individual soul, the fundamental irrationality of behavior, becoming as opposed to being, subjective choice instead of conventional behavior, concrete things above abstract doctrines, belief as action rather than assent to form and ritual, all expressed in orthodox vocabulary—a faith, in short, more pragmatic and idiosyncratic than traditional and doctrinal—was too much an anomaly in Victorian England to be fully grasped. In a profound sense, he worshipped a homemade God. No other was possible to him. It was his way of translating religious conventions into a living faith. He explored the full implications of this faith in all his religious poetry.

Therefore it is no longer necessary to apologize for an interest in Robert Browning's professed belief in God. But as this brief introduction has indicated, Browning's religion cannot be approached from any traditional point of view. He fits neatly into no pigeonhole. To discover the content of his words—*God,* for example—we must examine contextually each separate use. No one has used religious language's multivalence more effectively or ambiguously than he. Aware of the imprecision of words in conveying life's deepest emotions, he did not hesitate to give them individual, even idiosyncratic, definitions. Nevertheless, a definite pattern emerges in Browning's poems which indicates how he believed. That pattern outlines the amazingly simple faith of the one often called the most complexly cerebral Victorian poet. In an almost businesslike fashion, he early in life surveyed his intellectual and religious milieu, pronounced it bankrupt, entrusted his personal assets to his own ingenuity rather than to accepted authorities, tested his decisions against all possible alternatives, and never turned his eyes from his self-made goals. Finding no given order in his universe, he thrust himself upon it. Making himself the norm for, rather than the exception to, the universe, he appropriated the necessary God-language to consecrate his views. The pattern of Browning's belief, then, can be simply expressed in directional terms. He begins with an *inward* existential posture, trusting always in his perceptions, conceptions, and intuitions as final arbiters in religious decisions; he projects himself *outward* into other personalities, testing and justifying his existential decisions as he sees them replayed in the lives of his characters in the dramatic monologues; he propels himself *forward* in time, finding himself ontologically a dynamic, struggling, goal-oriented being; and he extends himself *upward,* sensing in his own being evidence for transcendence which can never be explained but must be expressed in God-language.

This pattern prevails in his religious thinking from *Pauline* to *Asolando.* It might be convenient to think of his poems as falling into three periods. The first, his *exploratory* period, would include *Pauline* (1833), *Paracelsus* (1835) and *Sordello* (1840). In these poems, the real Robert Browning speaks, although he employs a thin dramatic veil in the latter two poems. By 1840, he has defined his religious and intellectual concerns and has found the dramatic technique for expressing them. He is ready for his *experimental* stage, the period of the dramatic monologues, which operate like objective experiments to test the hypotheses which he has developed during his exploratory period. This second stage extends from *Pippa Passes* (1841), the first of the *Bells and Pomegranates* series, through *The Ring and the Book* (1868–1869), and includes Browning's best dramatic monologues and his most objective presentations of his religious ideas. The final period could be labelled *expository* and includes all the work after *The Ring and the Book.* In these poems, the poet moves out from behind the dramatic mask and speaks directly, often imposing his ideas upon his poems, no longer struggling to maintain dramatic tension. He says little that is new in this period, and the old that he repeats he often belabors with unrelenting garrulity. These later poems almost function as commentaries to the dramatic poems. In this work they will be so treated, borrowed occasionally for additional insight into the poems of the first two periods, but not studied specifically for their own sakes, except in the discussion of Browning's hope. The pattern of Browning's faith which is established in the exploratory period will be traced through the experimental stage. It will soon become evident that Browning assumed his religious attitude very early in his career and did not change it. His turbulent years of rejection of the Dissenting faith, worship of Shelley (with its attending vegetarianism and atheism), and gradual return to a redefined independent religious position, which he recounts in *Pauline,* occurred before he published his first poem. What we meet in his poems is a remarkable consistency of approach which seemed satisfactory to the young poet and the old expositor alike.

The Exploratory Period

Robert Browning called *Pauline* "A Fragment of a Confession." As an acknowledged autobiographical poem, it offers an ideal study in the young poet's use of religious language. The religious problem in the poem is so pervasive that his most recent biographer expands the subtitle to describe it as "a confession to the God to whom he is returning."[1] But with this assertion, our search for the meaning of Browning's faith begins. Who is the God to whom *Pauline*'s poet returns? Does this very personal poem offer clues to pierce the dramatic shield of his later monologues? It does, but not explicitly. Lacking an organized structure, *Pauline* undulates like a sea of contraries, floating from spirit to body, hope to despair, courage to resignation, stability to change, self to others, feeling to fact, and impulse to duty with the indirection of stream-of-consciousness writing. All this movement makes the identification of Browning's God difficult.

Perhaps the poem is not about God, or a return to God, at all. John Stuart Mill, the poem's first and most famous critic, does not even mention God in his denigrating review. Not God, but Browning, dominates—and a quite unattractive Browning at that: "With considerable poetic powers, the writer seems to be possessed with a more intense and morbid self-consciousness than I ever knew in any sane human being."[2] Regretting the poet's insensitive treatment of Pauline, who is but "a mere phantom" whom the "self-seeking and self-worshipping" poet addresses, Mill can only credit him with "the

1. Maisie Ward, *Robert Browning and His World: The Private Face, 1812–1861*, p. 36.
2. From Mill's notes for a review of *Pauline*. Reprinted in *Robert Browning: A Collection of Critical Essays*, edited by Philip Drew, p. 176.

psychological history of himself" which, he says, "is powerful and truthful—*truth-like* certainly. . . "[3] This early review obviously does not consider the poem a religious confessional, in spite of its God-language. What it does confess, according to Mill, is Browning's fascination with himself. Pauline is but an object to whom he speaks, not in order to communicate, but in order to listen to himself. She is just an excuse for his self-indulgence.

That Mill correctly read the poem, exposing the sensitive and egocentric young poet, seems certain from Browning's subsequent poems. *Pauline* is his last confessional. More objective poetry follows: *Paracelsus* adopts a dramatic structure, *Sordello* a narrative one.

The speaker in *Pauline* resembles the speakers in the later monologues, who talk in order to learn something about themselves. The monologues, as their name implies, are not conversations between people, but words from a person about the person to that person—all spoken in the presence of another. There is no sharing of confidences or exploring of ideas together; there is only self-exploration and justification. *Pauline,* in this respect, belongs with the dramatic monologues.

Browning refused until late in his life to grant his readers again such direct access to himself. He eagerly consigned *Pauline* to oblivion, where he hoped it would remain. He might have succeeded in forgetting it, had not Dante Gabriel Rossetti, Browning's great Pre-Raphaelite admirer (who so treasured *Sordello* that he insisted on reading great quantities of it at a time to his brothers in the movement), found *Pauline* in the British Museum and recognized that the unsigned poem was written by *Sordello's* poet. So, finally, Browning reluctantly included it in his 1868 collected works, attempting to gloss over its confessional character by stating that it, along with his other works, was "dramatic in principle."

Browning's reluctance to republish *Pauline* and his later insistence upon his right to privacy suggest that he may have confessed more than he intended. Certainly, *Pauline* reveals the method of arriving at religious truth which will dominate his poetry for the rest of his long life. So intense is the young speaker, and so earnest are his confessions of faith in God, that it would be quite easy to read the poem as Miss Ward does, as a "confession to the God to whom he is returning." Perhaps, however, the best approach might be to borrow Browning's defense of his *Sordello* as an explanation of *Pauline*: "My stress lay

3. *Ibid.*

on the incidents in the development of a soul: little else is worth the study."[4] In *Pauline,* the soul, preponderant and pretentious though it sounds, is quite immature and undeveloped. The speaker is a young man awakening to self-awareness, not yet fully certain who he is. Missing are the coherence and discipline—and the reticence—of mature thought; in their places are energy, emotion, and the extreme vacillations of youth. Every other presence represents strength, security, independence—all qualities that he lacks. So he reaches out to each of them in turn: Pauline, Shelley, God (concretely represented in Christ), then back to Pauline, and, at the end of the poem, ambiguously to both God and Shelley. In these perplexed appeals to others, he expresses a vague awareness of four possible claims to his ultimate concern, that regulating and stabilizing allegiance which is religious faith. The faithful and loving Pauline, the aesthetic and philosophical Shelley, the omniscient yet merciful God, and the powerful longing of his own soul all present themselves as worthy of his devotion.

He has little trouble dismissing himself from any claims to sufficiency: he has experienced the futility of autonomy, which leads only to decay and finally to despair. He cannot fulfill his needs: he wants guidance and companionship; he needs to worship. If his tone sounds hysterical, it is because he cannot reflect dispassionately about himself. Self-discovery is no academic exercise. If Pauline, Shelley, and God seem but nebulous shadows cast across the poet's pathway, it is because the poet has not yet discovered that only in clearly seeing them can he know himself. In this poem, they remain simply means to an end. They are objects; he is the only subject. Consequently, he struggles in lonely confusion, consuming rather than communing in friendship.

From the opening lines, the speaker's preoccupation with his needs prevails:

> Pauline, mine own, bend o'er me—thy soft breast
> Shall pant to mine—bend o'er me—thy sweet eyes,
> And loosened hair and breathing lips, and arms
> Drawing me to thee—these build up a screen
> To shut me in with thee, and from all fear;
> So that I might unlock the sleepless brood
> Of fancies from my soul.

[1–7]

---

4. Browning to Milsand, 1863. Quoted in DeVane, *Handbook,* p. 73.

Dependency, fear, and withdrawal from the world characterize the speaker. He subordinates himself to Pauline, who must bend down to him and draw him up to her. She is the superior one, protective and aggressive; he is inferior, protected and submissive. Subsequent lines further illustrate this unequal relationship. With almost litanylike repetitions, the poet confesses his inferiority. Yet he cannot accept his condition. Aware of his straining energy and his potential for growth, he searches for something or someone to give his life direction:

> I am a watcher whose eyes have grown dim
> With looking for some star which breaks on him
> Altered and worn and weak and full of tears.
>
> [227–229]

Not by nature submissive, he has deliberately rejected independence because, having exercised his own freedom, he has experienced its tendency toward anarchy. In spite of his almost overpowering self-consciousness, he has learned that without external guidance he lacks direction, unable to distinguish good from bad, unable to direct the emotional turbulence within. So he rejects autonomy: "No more of the past! / I have too trusted my own lawless wants" (937–938). His bitter final self-condemnation stands in poignant contrast with the central portion of the poem. There the poet imaginatively feasts himself in self-adoration, envisioning his soul as a temple filled with troops of shadows hailing him as kind and serving his every creative impulse. But self-worship only intensifies loneliness and emphasizes the vanity of trust in one's powers.

What can a man do when he has experienced the boundaries of his strength? If he cannot be king of his own being, to whom shall he give his allegiance? He responds to three other claims: Pauline, his love; Shelley, his hero; and God. His attitude toward all three is the same. In each case, he stresses his inferiority to them—not in neurotic self-rejection but in an effort at honest self-appraisal. He needs them as exemplars; he desires their companionship. Realizing that he cannot live and grow alone, he tentatively allies himself with them—but not to serve them. Their causes are secondary; their importance is their service to him. Although he has consciously rejected personal autonomy, he subconsciously yields authority to no one. His professions of inferiority repeated so regularly sound hollow.

The poet tells us very little about Pauline. He assures us she is "so good, / So calm"—in contrast to the passionate and morally stained

31

poet. She loves him and receives from him in return "not love but faith," as he promises: "And I look to thee and I trust in thee." Emphasizing the moral and spiritual distance between them, in every way he submits himself to her:

> Hand in hand, we will go
> I with thee, even as a child—love's slave
> Looking no farther than his liege commands.
>
> [947–949]

Stated simply, the poet promises "And now, my Pauline, I am thine forever!" but the words seem to mean "Leave me not."

When he addresses Shelley, the poet's genuine admiration bursts forth, but his self-preoccupation still prevails. His praise of Shelley is sung in language appropriate for the deity: "His whom all honour," "thy majesties," "mighty works," "as on a throne," "with all thy dim creations gathered round," "as one should worship long a sacred spring." But mingled with these praises are numerous references to himself and, as usual, they are self-deprecating, purposely widening the gulf between the worshipped and the worshipper: "For I have nought in common with him." He finds in Shelley the peaceful security, guidance, and strength that he knows in Pauline. And, in his final apostrophe to Shelley, after professing his belief in "God and truth / And love," he confesses his continuing dependence upon Shelley in language little different from his plea to Pauline to "leave me not":

> I would lean on thee!
> Thou must be ever with me, most in gloom
> If such must come, but chiefly when I die,
> For I seem, dying, as one going in the dark
> To fight a giant: but live thou for ever,
> And be to all what thou hast been to me!
>
> [1023–1028]

Turning from the poet's relation with Pauline and Shelley to that with God, we discover the same outward movement from a felt need to a reliance upon someone to fulfill that need. The nature of God is not his concern. God's importance is in assisting the poet to fulfill himself. Attempting to discover his essence, he reduces himself to what he believes is the core of his being:

I am made up of an intensest life,
Of a most clear idea of consciousness
Of self, distinct from all its qualities,
From all affections, passions, feelings, powers;
And thus far it exists, if tracked, in all:
But linked, in me, to self-supremacy,
Existing as a centre to all things,
Most potent to create and rule and call
Upon all things to minister to it;
And to a principle of restlessness
Which would be all, have, see, know, taste, feel, all—
This is myself; and I should thus have been
Though gifted lower than the meanest soul.

[268–280]

Here, then, is a human being: intensely alive, clearly aware of self, possessing but not dependent upon "affections, passions, feelings, powers" for being; autonomous, and omnivorous—devouring all that the senses find. In addition to these properties common to all men, the poet possesses "an imagination which / Has been a very angel." A personality so dynamic could easily, as the poet confesses, destroy himself. Hence, an organizing aim, a "lode-star" is needed:

As I look back, I see that I have halted
Or hastened as I looked toward the star—
A need, a trust, a yearning after God.

[292–295]

Again the resemblance to his relationship with Pauline and Shelley is apparent: he yearns after God as he yearned after them. And, as he feels compelled to confess his inferiority to Pauline ("I felt despair could never live by thee") and his faithlessness to Shelley ("I am not what I have been to thee") so here he must confess his apostacy, weakness, and doubt. Much later he returns to the same theme: "And what is that I hunger for but God?" Then, having named the object of his desire, he pleads:

My God, my God, let me for once look on thee
As though nought else existed, we alone!
And as creation crumbles, my soul's spark
Expands till I can say, —Even from myself
I need thee and I feel thee and I love thee.

33

I do not plead my rapture in thy works
For love of thee, nor that I feel as one
Who cannot die: but there is that in me
Which turns to thee, which loves or which should love.

[822–830]

Through the repetition of "my," "me," "I," and "myself" in these lines devoted to God, the location of the poet's proof for God's existence becomes evident: God exists for the poet because his existence demands that God exist. The intense subjectivity of the poem, with only casually vague references to time, place, or event, prepares the reader to accept the poet's feeling. Metaphysical, cosmological, teleological or any other traditional arguments for God are irrelevant. Psychological proof suffices. Of course, the question of God's reality is not at issue here. The poet simply accepts God's existence with the same assurance as that with which he accepts Pauline and Shelley. No satisfactory rational explanation can be advanced for his adoration; yet the soul, "knit round/ As with a charm by sin and lust and pride" still reaches outward, unable to do otherwise. His very being demands Someone to worship.

Nothing more conclusive can be said about God than one's own nature can assert. Thus belief in God can never be equated with knowledge of God; in fact, even belief cannot be equated with absolute certainty. On this issue, Browning differed decisively from Cardinal Newman. Reading in the *Apologia Pro Vita Sua* Newman's statement that "'he is as convinced of the existence of God'—an individual, not an external force merely—'as of his own existence,'" Browning demurred: "I believe he deceives himself and that no sane man has ever had, with mathematical exactness, equal conviction on those two points—though the approximation to equality may be in any degree short of that."[5] What Browning can be certain of, as *Pauline* repeatedly expresses, is the reality of the individual soul. Nothing else is so real. Less certain, but nonetheless strong, is his inclination to worship, his need for Someone. Thus he speaks of God not so much as the Omnipotent, Omniscient, Omnipresent Deity of theology, but as the One who satisfies his personal hunger. In speaking of God, he moves, seemingly without knowledge of his transition, to a description of himself in Christ's company. As if unable to remain on an abstract

5 Browning to Julia Wedgwood, June 27, 1864. *Robert Browning and Julia Wedgwood.* edited by Richard Curle, pp. 12–13.

level, he makes concrete his ontological need to talk about God by
seizing upon the central events of Christ's life and participating vicariously in them:

> Oft have I stood by thee—
> Have I been keeping lonely watch with thee
> In the damp night by weeping Olivet,
> Or leaning on thy bosom, proudly less,
> Or dying with thee on the lonely cross,
> Or witnessing thine outburst from the tomb.

> [849–854]

We are reminded of his need for companionship with Pauline and
Shelley. He may himself have felt the similarity, for a few lines later
he says abruptly, "And now, my Pauline, I am thine for ever!" This
picture of the poet and Christ, with the poet inferior and dependent,
able to die with Christ but only observe his resurrection, depicts precisely the attitude the poet assumes with Pauline and Shelley. The
importance is not in Christ's sacrifice and resurrection nor what these
events signify about the nature of God or God's will, but in the reassur-
ance they give the poet, satisfying his longing. Even when he vows to
give up everything himself "to believe and humbly teach the faith /
In suffering and poverty and shame," he reveals his motive in his
only stipulation: "Only believing he is not unloved." His faith depends
upon pragmatic results. He makes God, as he has made Pauline and
Shelley, his servants.

This reading of *Pauline* suggests several facts about Browning's
faith.

1. The most obvious characteristic of the poem is the self-
consciousness which Mill found. Never do the other personalities really
hold his attention; never does he attempt to know them better. He
wants to be loved, not to love, Acutely conscious of his incompleteness,
he reaches outward to grasp and appropriate to himself others who
can help him reach fulfillment. He is incapable of experiencing a
true I-Thou relationship; rather, in his egocentricity he remains at
the mechanical I-It level, using but not relating personally to others.
There is no awareness of the uniqueness of Pauline as a person;
he regards Shelley as exemplar, but not as a person. Both of these
personalities remain shadowy and peripheral to the poet's ego. God,
too, remains object. He is servant of the poet's longings, not Lord
of his life. The poem begins and ends with the poet. There is no

movement from self-consciousness to other-consciousness, in spite of the dangers the poet recognizes in self-serving.

This primacy of the soul is the key to understanding Browning's faith. Although it is interesting to study the basic doctrines of the Dissenting faith in which he grew up, or the various higher critical or liberal movements to which Browning responded, *Pauline* demonstrates that his faith was so subjective, his presuppositions so existential, that he placed little confidence in these traditional sources of religious authority. Fascinated by human personality, especially his own, he probed and tested to find its essence. Anything which did not relate to himself, satisfying either a desire or a need, or revealing some new truth about his life, had no real significance. He claimed and modified to his specifications whatever he needed and ignored all else. The essence of his faith, then, cannot be discovered through an examination of any of the religious movements which touched his life: they only touched; they did not penetrate.

2. Implied in the first conclusion is a second: To assert the primacy of the self-conscious soul suggests that the soul is not alone in the world. Rather, it exists in a crowded universe and finds itself only in relation to its surroundings. In *Pauline,* the poet constantly moves about, measuring himself against others, using them as reflectors or standards, weighing himself in the balances of their personalities and achievements. The soul is social, dependent, untrustworthy apart from some external standards and guides. It must not be imprisoned in its sensory experience. "It will not rest / In its clay prison, this most narrow sphere." It transcends the intellect: within is "strange impulse, tendency, desire, / Which nowise I account for nor explain." The intellect's inability to explain the soul's urges does not remove them. They must be acknowledged; the poet is "bound to trust / All feelings equally, to hear all sides."

How does one hear all sides of himself? Browning's way was to reach outward, toward other personalities (real or imagined), objectifying and evaluating his ideas and aspects of his personality. Pauline, Shelley, and God (and God-in-Christ), though of much less importance than the speaker, are nonetheless vital to the poet's self-understanding. They are thus intimately associated with the foils of the later monologues, who perform these measuring and reflecting functions for the speakers. Read in this way, the movement from the autobiographical *Pauline* to the mature dramatic monologues does not seem so drastic as some have assumed it to be. Nor do critics need to resort to the theory of a brokenhearted Browning crushed by Mill's review into abandoning this form for more objective poetry. The passive but essential roles of these reflectors in *Pauline* differ hardly at all from those of Festus in *Paracelsus,* Gigadibs in *Bishop Blougram's Apology,* or Protus in *Cleon.* They provide an objective reality against which the subjective impulses of the soul can be measured.

Browning's recognition of the role of the objective is at the heart of his poetic theory—and of his religious conviction. This fact in part explains the frequency with which his several characters speak of God. Through them, he objectifies elements of his faith, then subjects them to experiments in living situations. Beginning with the inner testimony of the soul, he moves outward and incarnates that testimony in his characters. The confessional of *Pauline* becomes the dramatic monologue, retaining the basic soul-and-foil settings throughout his career, symbolizing his understanding of the subjective-objective nature of faith.

3. The third fact about Browning's faith suggested by *Pauline* is found in his repetition of words like "aim," "end," and "choice," which imply a forward thrust. Clearly the poet is searching not only for personal relationships but also for a goal toward which to direct his life, offering organization to his impulses, structure to his values, and meaning to his life. Although he turns to his past to trace his development, he refuses to be bound by the dictates of his history. He is neither a determinist nor a predestinarian. On the other hand, neither is he a totally free agent, since complete freedom enslaves oneself. Browning affirms freedom, but as a free person he must find his "lode-star," his master—his God. In *Pauline* the final goal is not found. The poem's incoherence reflects the poet's indecision. He does not know where he is going.

4. One final fact about Browning's faith can be derived from *Pauline.* In spite of obvious similarities to Browning's treatment of Pauline and Shelley, God is not exactly just another personality. It is true that, in speaking of God, in one passage, the poet slips into a description of Christ, as incarnate deity. Yet for Browning to speak of incarnation is to limit God to the human—the knowable, tangible, immediate. He refuses to confine God to the knowable. The poet's soul "has strange impulse, tendency, desire, / Which nowise I account for nor explain." But these impulses are real: "They live, / Referring to some state of life unknown." Unable to explain all that his soul experiences, he must nonetheless find some words to acknowledge them. He can use certain words because they have attained at least a consensus meaning. Browning thus speaks of *truth* or *love* or *joy* in the confidence

that he is conveying some generally accepted definition. His definition of *God,* however, although still carrying orthodox overtones, conveys mystery more than meaning to Browning. It is apparent that in the poet's final apostrophe to Shelley, "Sun-treader, I believe in God and truth / And love," *love* and *truth* refer to life's tangible realities and *God* to its ineffable mysteries. *Love* and *truth* are words whose definitions everyone feels he knows because he uses them daily. He knows them, that is, until he attempts to define them, then all definitions of *love* and *truth* become abstractions, inadequate to convey their total significance. If this is true of such common words which *do* have definite meanings in concrete situations, what can be said of the meaning of the word *God?* Browning avoids the problem by ignoring the question. He does not try to define *God.* In *Pauline,* at least, *God* refers to the poet's sense of transcendence, of an existence of that beyond himself which is somehow like, yet terribly unlike, himself.

In the strange context of a love letter to Elizabeth Barrett in 1846, Browning explains his use of religious language. The letter insists explicitly as strongly as *Pauline* does implicitly in the primacy of human individuality, and proves that Browning was very much aware of the anthropomorphic character of his God-language. Decrying the inhumane treatment Elizabeth was receiving from her jealously protective father, Browning plunges headlong into a description of the uses of language:

> But I do hold it the most stringent duty of all who can, to stop
> a condition, a relation of one human being to another which
> God never allowed to exist between Him and ourselves. *Trees*
> live and die, if you please, and accept will for a law—but with us,
> all commands surely refer to a previously-implanted conviction
> in ourselves of their rationality and justice. Or why declare that
> "the Lord is holy, just and good" unless there is recognized
> an independent conception of holiness and goodness, to which
> the subsequent assertion is referable? "You know what holiness
> is, what it is to be good? Then, He *is* that"—not, "*that* is so—
> because *he* is that"; though, of course, when once the converse
> is demonstrated, this, too, follows, and may be urged for prac-
> tical purposes. All God's urgency, so to speak, is on the *justice*
> of his judgments, *rightness* of his rule; Yet why? one might ask

—if one does believe that the rule *is* his; why ask further?—
Because, his is a "reasonable service," once for all.[6]

Written in Browning's typically convoluted prose style, the argument threatens to lose the reader in a welter of words. Four facts of Browning's use of God-language are clear, however, The first is that a belief in God is assumed, although He is not explained. The second is that the human mind possesses sufficient power and knowledge to make moral judgments; even spiritual commands are given in reasonable language. Third, the attributes assigned to God are adjectives of human experience, concepts men regularly use of themselves. God-language, although referring to transcendence, is still the limited medium of human vocabulary. Fourth, for pragmatic reasons, God-language sounds as if human virtues are prized because they are attributes of God and not, more correctly, because, valued as human virtues, they are attributed to God. Browning's religious language, like his arguments for God's existence, begins with the personal and human and moves upward.

These four conclusions which *Pauline* suggests about Browning's faith (its existential basis, its experimental method of objectifying the subjective, its goal-orientation, and its use of anthropomorphic language for a transcendent reality) provide standards against which to judge subsequent expressions of his faith.

The religious language of *Paracelsus* reveals the same components of belief found in *Pauline*, with some important modifications. Superficially, the two poems appear quite dissimilar. *Paracelsus* is technically superior, demonstrating Browning's growing control over his material. There are no embarrassingly personal disclosures. *Pauline's* tortuous stream-of-consciousness style has given way to a neatly organized five-act structure which moves logically from Paracelsus's announced aspirations in the opening scene to his final intuition of the truth in the death scene. The supporting characters are more clearly realized in the later poem, although they remain types rather than individualized personalities. Dialogue has replaced monologue. In other words, Browning appears successfully to have disguised himself.

In several important respects, however, *Paracelsus* is merely an amplification of *Pauline*. Both poems focus upon the development of a soul, with internal struggles and tensions observing external action. Both portray Promethean personalities struggling within the

6. *The Letters of Robert Browning and Elizabeth Barrett Browning 1845–1846*, edited by Robert Barrett Browning, II, 414–415.

limitations of human finitude, seeking a way to burst through them—Pauline's poet, through reliance upon other personalities; Paracelsus, by personal dynamism. Both are obsessed with the importance of goals—the poet, to find one for his life; Paracelsus, to fulfill his. Both the poet and Paracelsus fail to realize any genuine reciprocal relationship with another person. They use, rather than love, their fellows. Both speak confusingly but frequently of God. It is impossible not to infer that in *Paracelsus* Browning has returned to the unfinished business of *Pauline,* treating more dramatically in the later poem the questions he considered in the earlier one. Thus the real subject remains the same, although the point of view shifts from the "I" of *Pauline* to the third person of *Paracelsus.*

The use of God-language in the poems suggests another shift. *Paracelsus* appears to be an extremely religious poem, dominated by a quest for and conversations about God and God's will. In some of the conversations between Paracelsus and Festus, the meaning of God's will is seriously debated. However, much of the God-language may be as much a disguise as the dramatic structure and characterization of the poem. *Paracelsus* often uses *God* as nothing more than a label for his drives or a rationale for his behavior. He effectively clothes his selfishness in the language of piety. Consequently, the reader finds himself questioning the content of the God-language. Does Browning mean anything definite by *God*? Is Paracelsus in part a language experiment, with Browning testing *God* to determine whether it has any independent meaning? Is it to be read as a noun or as an adjective modifying man?

From the opening scene, Paracelsus makes explicit the primacy of the self which is implicit throughout *Pauline.* Paracelsus is more aggressive, dominant—"masculine"—than Pauline's poet, but his extroversion is no less self-centered than the painful introversion of the poet. Confident of his powers and eager to test them, Paracelsus discovers that his "own aim's extent" is

> to comprehend the works of God,
> And God himself, and all God's intercourse
> with human mind.

> [I. 533–535]

Exhilarated by this goal, he promises: "I go to prove my soul!" His goal to know everything is a God-given commission:

> I profess no other share
> In the selection of my lot, than this
> My ready answer to the will of God
> Who summons me to be his organ.
>
> [292–295]

In this opening section, however, the confusion of the will of God with the will of Paracelsus becomes apparent. Asserting that faith "should be acted on as best we may," Paracelsus ventures "to submit / My plan, in lack of better, for pursuing / The path with God's will seems to authorize." The initiative here is with Paracelsus, not God; the path in these lines only seems to be authorized by God. In the absence of divine proof of a commission, he resorts to paradox:

> The sovereign proof
> That we devote ourselves to God, is seen
> In living just as though no God there were.
>
> [I. 186–188]

But to live as if there were no God is to define oneself with reference to no one else. No one can claim to have been made in the image of God if he lives "as though no God there were." He cannot even act the Promethean role and steal fire from a God who is not there. In this sense, then, Paracelsus is not so much a Promethean character modeled after Shelley's hero, as he is an existentialist hero, alone in a universe, condemned to freedom, defining from his existence what it means to be a man. By recognizing no higher authority, Paracelsus can readily speak of God's will as his own. He can argue later:

> Why ever make man's good distinct from God's?
> Or, finding they are one, why dare mistrust?
> Who shall succeed if not one pledged like me?
>
> [I. 789–791]

Paracelsus's arguments in this first section ring truer when he claims to live "as though no God there were" than when he hides his egoism behind allusions to God.

Throughout the poem, Paracelsus pursues his goal to know all. As he vacillates between exhilaration and despondency, his God-language reflects his moods. In prosperity, he confidently represents God as his partner in his endeavors, although he never again can assume the fully authoritative manner of speaking of God as in the first section. In adversity, God's separation is more real than his pre-

41

sence. He is bewildered by the God who "may take pleasure in confounding pride / By hiding secrets with the scorned and base." He cries out to God in his misery: "O God, the despicable heart of us!" Like Pauline's poet, in his weakness, he exalts the one to whom he looks for deliverance. At the end of his meeting with Aprile, sharing with the poet a sense of weakness ("We are weak dust"), Paracelsus cries out to both Aprile and God,

> Love me henceforth, Aprile, while I learn
> To love; and, merciful God, forgive us both!

[II. 618–619]

Later, in Basil, the one who began his quest declaring all truth to be "within ourselves" now must confess to Festus:

> Well, then: you know my hopes;
> I am assured, at length, those hopes were vain;
> That truth is just as far from me as ever.

[III. 500–502]

Festus sympathetically begins to answer him, "Dear Aureole, can it be my fears were just? / God wills not." But Parcelsus impatiently cuts short his speech in a tirade which contradicts his earlier assurance of his knowledge of God's will:

> Now, 't is this I most admire—
> The constant talk men of your stamp keep up
> Of God's will, as they style it; one would swear
> Man had but merely to uplift his eye,
> And see the will in question charactered
> On the heaven's vault. 't is hardly wise to moot
> Such topics: doubts are many and faith is weak.
> I know as much of any will of God
> As knows some dumb and tortured brute what Man,
> His stern lord, wills from the perplexing blows
> That plague him every way; but there, of course,
> Where least he suffers, longest he remains—
> My case; and for such reasons I plod on,
> Subdued but not convinced. I know as little
> Why I deserve to fail, as why I hoped
> Better things in my youth. I simply know
> I am no master here, but trained and beaten
> Into the path I tread.

[III. 510–527]

A discouraged man acknowledges his distance from God. There is no denial of God's existence, only denial of any clear communication of his will to men. Accepting the reality of a God, wanting to receive "some feeble glimmering token that God views / And may approve" his pennance, he still finds that "God's intimations rather fail / In clearness than in energy," and that he has lost his earlier certainty about God's designs for his life. Nonetheless he will not abandon the only purpose to which he is committed: "I must know!" To know everything, he will use anything—even God:

> Would God translate me to his throne, believe
> That I should only listen to his word
> To further my own aim!
>
> [III. 707–709]

Gone is the assumption that "my own aim" and God's will are one.

In Alsatia, Paracelsus aspires again. This time he determines to "seek to know and to enjoy at once, / Not one without the other as before." Confidence of God's involvement is gone; what remains, as he later admits, is just his subjective evidence of God:

> I lapse back into youth, and take again
> My fluttering pulse for evidence that God
> Means good to me, will make my cause his own.
>
> [IV. 400–402]

Faithful Festus, horrified by Paracelsus's new devotion to dissipation, provides the perfect foil for Paracelsus's passionate vacillations. Festus simply accepts that there is a God who has revealed his will, which believers are to follow, through his institutions. He reminds Paracelsus that "God's service is established here / And he determines fit." To Festus God is always Lord, always Love: "God, Thou are love! I build my faith on that." God is the object of worship; He is not servant of any human being. He manifested himself to mankind, providing values and standards for behavior. Festus is unable to believe that God will not save Paracelsus, in spite of his arrogant rejection of God's laws. For Aprile, love meant creativity, beauty, perfection. For Festus, love—and therefore God—means mercy, longsuffering, forgiveness, steadfastness. Festus's ability to enter sympathetically into the lives of Michal and Paracelsus has led him to a less idiosyncratic understanding of his God; for Festus, God can be other than his own desires or needs projected outward. For Paracelsus, such objectivity is impossible. Festus exposes the unreliability of any of Paracelsus's language about God.

In the final scene, the growing contrast between the God-language of Paracelsus and that of Festus reaches its climax. The strength of the apparently weak Festus and the weakness of the powerful Paracelsus are brought into sharp relief. Festus, still trusting in the God of love, attends his dying friend and humbly prays for his salvation, revealing his selfless love. Beliving always that "man is made for weakness," Festus's prayer demonstrates that weakness is strength when it loses itself in devotion for another. Even a weak man can approach God, when he loves. But Festus would not call this daring so great a feat, since God by definition is love, mercy, and forgiveness. To such a God, a prayer offered in love must be granted in love.

His God is not Paracelsus's, however. His goal has not been to serve God, but to gain God's "great approval." When he approaches death, Paracelsus is cognizant of God's superior power, admitting that he cannot attain that power through striving, even attributing to God mercy and goodness—yet he again seeks to make God subservient. The emphasis remains upon himself, not God. No longer feeling the "supernatural consciousness of strength / Which fed my youth," he cries out in agony,

> Lost, lost! Thus things are ordered here! God's creatures,
> And yet he takes no pride in us!—none, none!
>
> [V. 272–273]

With this forward vision that has driven him relentlessly through life in pursuit of knowledge, he looks at death beyond the "ordered here" to another opportunity for further pursuit:

> Truly there needs another life to come!
> If this be all—(I must tell Festus that)
> And other life await us now—for one,
> I say 't is a poor cheat, a stupid bungle,
> A wretched failure. I, for one, protest
> Against it, and I hurl it back with scorn.
>
> [V. 274–279]

A death without further life is inconceivable to him. He whose life has been driven by purpose cannot conceive of death without purpose. Death's purpose must be to provide access to further life.

In the final moments of his life, Paracelsus feels himself filled with divine power. He is granted intuitional insight into the truth so long denied him in the midst of his struggles to know all. Leaving his deathbed, dressed once again as a don, he delivers his last lecture, confident finally that "here God speaks to men through me." God's message according to Paracelsus is that his life has not been in vain, that in doing one's best "praise rises, and will rise for ever," and that "we have to live alone to set forth well / God's praise." Paracelsus now knows that he himself has been "not all so valueless," although he too soon forgot the time he vowed himself to man. Unlike most men who amble aimlessly through life, he was born to the task he pursued:

> But this was born in me; I was made so;
> Thus much timed saved: the feverish appetites,
> The tumult of unproved desire, the unaimed
> Uncertain yearnings, aspirations blind,
> Distrust, mistake, and all that ends in tears
> Were saved me; thus I entered on my course.
>
> [V. 622–627]

He knew his share of doubt and trouble on his quest. But thanks to his purposeful life, he now can speak boldly of his understanding of God:

> I knew, I felt, (perception unexpressed,
> Uncomprehended by our narrow thought,
> But somehow felt and known in every shift
> And change in the spirit,—nay, in every pore
> Of the body, even,)—what God is, what we are.
> What life is—how God tastes an infinite joy
> In infinite ways—one everlasting bliss,
> From whom all being emanates, all power
> Proceeds; in whom is life for evermore,
> Yet whom existence in its lowest form
> Includes; where dwells enjoyment there is he:
> With still a flying point of bliss remote,
> A happiness in store afar, a sphere
> Of distant glory in full view; thus climbs
> Pleasure its heights for ever and for ever.
> The centre-fire heaves underneath the earth,
> And the earth changes like a human face;

45

The molten ore bursts up among the rocks,
Winds into the stone's heart, outbranches bright
In hidden mines, spots barren river-beds,
Crumbles into fine sand where sunbeams bask—
God joys therein.

[V. 638–659]

Beginning as always with his own feelings, Paracelsus infers that God, like himself, finds joy in variety, movement, and progress. He identifies as the source of all being and all power; in fact, he includes all life and all time and is found in all existence, even "in its lowest form." He is thus transcendent and immanent, source of life and life itself, the creator of the universe who infuses every particle of it. He is in Aprile's words, "the perfect poet / Who in his person acts his own creations." The omnipresent God works through the variegated creatures of his handiwork toward the culmination of his earthly activities: man, who combines knowledge and love with power. These are the qualities of the superior race. Nature's work concluded with man's creation, whose perfection, however, awaits his further development.

The importance of man does not stop here.
For these things tend still upward, progress is
The law of life, man is not Man as yet.

[V. 742–743]

Darkness still prevails, with only an occasional star among men to dispel the darkness. Not until "all mankind like is perfected" can man rest. For as all nature has travailed in creation and evolution, so does man strain toward further development:

But in completed man begins anew
A tendency to God. Prognostics told
Man's near approach; so in man's self arises
August anticipations, symbols, types
Of a dim splendour ever on before
In that eternal circle life pursues.
For men begin to pass their nature's bound,
And find new hopes and cares which fast supplant
Their proper joys and griefs; they grow too great
For narrow creeds of right and wrong, which fade
Before the unmeasured thirst for good: while peace
Rises within them ever more and more.

[V. 722–783]

Biological development is succeeded by ethical and spiritual growth. Man has not yet attained. Like Paracelsus, he has aspired but failed. Yet in that failure and imperfection is hope, and in hope is man's essence: "While hope and fear and love shall keep thee man!" Paracelsus had failed to understand that to have total knowledge would make him like God, for there would be nothing left to strive and hope for. The power he had "sought for man, seemed God's." He who began his quest in the assurance of the unity of his own will and God's will now realizes that man can never be God, can never know all God's purposes. On this note, and with a panegyric on love, Paracelsus dies.

This review of the God-language in Paracelsus reveals the same religious sensibility found in *Pauline*:

1. Overpowering every consideration is the primacy of self. Although references to God, nature, and general human welfare abound, Paracelsus subordinates them all to his purposes. Acting as if there were no God, he assumes the existential posture and defines all mankind by his personal standards. The complete renaissance man, Paracelsus would comprehend all knowledge and, through that knowledge, have all power. His is no theocentric universe. The kingdom of man has come, and God is his servant.

But the existentialist posture is insufficient. For all his strength of passion and personality, and all his indomitable egoism, his aspiration fails. Through his failure, Paracelsus experiences finitude. He dare not challenge the universe alone.

2. Shelley, Pauline, and God provide objectifying reflectors, standards and comrades for *Pauline*'s poet; Festus and Aprile perform these functions for Paracelsus. Anchoring his faith in his own feelings, Paracelsus moves repeatedly and wildly between arrogant and despondent moods. His concept of God varies accordingly. His professions of faith cannot be trusted. His ego is so powerful and his God-concept is so uneffected that Paracelsus does not allow God an independent existence until the final scene. The stability and objectivity are found in the other characters, not in God. Aprile and Festus supplement the partial viewpoint of Paracelsus and enable the reader to see the whole. They also reflect the weaknesses in Paracelsus's autonomous subjectivity: Aprile's love reflects upon Paracelsus's loveless isolation; the steadfastness of Festus makes more obvious the wavering instability of Paracelsus. The poem's dialectic is so skillful that the reader is unable to adopt totally any of the characters' viewpoints. As usual with Browning, the truth resides in no one part, but in the whole

which transcends the sum of the parts. As Paracelsus finally learns, truth does not come through human intelligence alone. There is more to reality than human endeavor can know. Through the help of Aprile and Festus, Paracelsus can learn something, but not all. The subjective personality, though primary, is not all of reality. Through experimentation, discussion, confrontation, and intuition, one can apprehend truth which exists independent of the will of men.

3. Goal-orientation, so important in *Pauline,* is thoroughly tested in *Paracelsus.* Pauline's poet flounders in an ocean of possibilities, finally unable to discriminate among them and direct his life toward one goal. Paracelsus, however, epitomizes commitment; he has chosen his goal and pursues it vigorously. He will become "the greatest and most glorious man on earth." He has made his life "consist of one idea." As Aprile aspires to express artistically all aspects of reality, so Paracelsus would capture knowledge of all creation. Arrogant and misdirected as these goals may be, they give their adherents superhuman power and sustain them even in the darkest days of rejection and defeat.

Paracelsus views his life in retrospect as "mixed up" with the "storm of life":

> I am dying, Festus,
> And now that fast the storm of life subsides,
> I first perceive how great the whirl has been.
> I was calm then, who am so dizzy now—
> Calm in the thick of the tempest, but no less
> A partner of its motion and mixed up
> With its career.

[V. 471–477]

Motion, energy, variation—such have been his life. Such is all life. In the midst of the whirl, he was calmed by his drive for his goal, but he was defeated—an incomplete man incapable of knowing all about an unfinished universe. All nature, like himself, grows through struggle. The reality that Paracelsus would know is not the mechanical sameness of the "chain of being" which ordered the universe for so many centuries. Man cannot know all about a dynamic universe, because all has not yet happened. So men live in expectancy, looking toward the future in hope and wonder.

What men can know is that the purposeful energy of nature is analogous to man's being. As nature has been developing through epochs, so man can develop his soul by organizing his powerful energies. Nature's progress has not been random; it has moved from simple to complex, from material toward spiritual. Human life develops likewise when it focuses upon the future, moving purposefully toward the spiritual. Paracelsus, so wrong in so much, is correct in setting his goal so high that he has to marshall every resource to attain it. He has sinned in wanting to be like God; he has not sinned in wanting to be fully man. A greater sin would have been to refuse to choose, to reject his impulse to grow and learn.

Only at death does Paracelsus comprehend fully the purposiveness of nature and of human existence. Life has meaning; so must death. A man faces death unfinished; there is still more to experience, to perfect. Death surely must provide another opportunity for development—man's soul cries out for more time:

> And this is death: I understand it all.
> Now being waits me; new perceptions must
> Be born in me before I plunge therein;
> Which last is Death's affair; and while I speak,
> Minute by minute he is filling me
> With power; and while my foot is on the threshold
> Of boundless life—the doors unopened yet,
> All preparations not complete within—
> I turn new knowledge upon old events.
>
> [V. 499–507]

The hope which has carried him through life will sustain him in death. Life will follow death. The energy within him strains forward, coming from the future. He who lives by the future will die into the future, which calls him unto itself.

4. Although Paracelsus frequently appropriates God-language to express his needs and desires, as Pauline's poet does, he shares the earlier speaker's need to acknowledge phenomena he cannot explain. Paracelsus employs God-language in three distinct ways. The first usage includes all the conventional and somewhat meaningless applications of the word *God* as intensifier, metaphor, or expletive:

> God knows I need such!
>
> [III. 144]

> No mean trick
> He left untried, and truly well-nigh wormed
> All traces of God's finger out of him.
>
> [III. 115–117]

49

Stop o' God's name.

[III. 163]

Secondly, God is used adjectively. Men attribute to God the qualities which characterize themselves. Often God is a human adjective. Thus to Paracelsus, seeking to master all knowledge and trusting the power of his intellect, God is Mind:

God! Thou art mind! Unto the master-mind
Mind should be precious. Spare my mind alone!
All else I will endure . . .
Crush not my mind, dear God, though I be crushed!

[II. 229–231; 241]

God is an infinite Paracelsus. To the poet Aprile, "God is the perfect poet." To faithful, constant, loving Festus, God is Love. In these lines, at least, God is not an Absolute Being. He is either the projection of human qualities or an expression of human needs. He is an adjective.

The third use of *God*, however, is nominative. God is, and is more than mere anthropological projection. God defies explanation. To be transcendent and immanent, separate from, yet integral to nature—these are grammatical impossibilities. There are no precise human definitions for an illimitable reality. But the beating of his pulse and the vast yearnings of nature convince Paracelsus that there is more to himself than the merely human and more to nature than the natural. Published in 1835, twenty-four years before Darwin's *Origin of Species, Paracelsus* speaks of God in terms that seem to anticipate Darwin's evolutionary hypothesis. But there is a difference. Darwin limits his studies to nature, explaining evolutionary development as natural selection. Browning, convinced that nature has undergone such an evolution—and is still developing—explains it rather from within a neoplatonic framework, positing a Reality outside nature working on and through nature to realize its Ideas. These words should not be taken to imply a systematic philosophy or theology which the poetic words in *Paracelsus* cannot be made to support. They mean simply that Browning, contemplating the supernatural forces and purposeful energy of nature, could not dismiss them just because he found his language inadequate to express them. Browning cannot conceive of a nonteleological universe. Presupposing a purpose, he must assume One who purposes. He calls that one God.

Following *Paracelsus*, Browning adds no essentials to his faith.

Although he will frequently examine religious questions and amplify these early treatments, his basic approach to them will not vary. His third major poem (the last one in his exploratory period), *Sordello*, concentrating on problems of art rather than religion, does not offer *Paracelsus*'s copious examples of God-language. It is difficult to draw any definite conclusions from the few references to God—especially about a work whose author later confessed, according to a popular legend, "When the poem was written, two knew what it meant—God and Robert Browning. Now God alone knows!"[7] In this amazingly complex collage of ideas, Browning summarizes the thoughts of his twenty-eight years in language so condensed, so allusive, and so lacking in helpful transitions that he baffles the most discerning reader. Like *Sordello,* Browning

> left imagining, to try the stuff
> That held the imaged thing, and, let it writhe
> Never so fiercely, scarce allowed a tithe
> To reach the light—his Language. How he sought
> The cause, conceived a cure, and slow re-wrought
> That Language,—welding words into the crude
> Mass from the new speech round him, till a rude
> Armour was hammered out, in time to be
> Approved beyond the Roman panoply
> Melted to make it,—boots not
> . . . . . .
> Fond essay!
> Piece after piece that armour broke away,
> Because perceptions whole, like that he sought
> To clothe, reject so pure a work of thought
> As language: thought may take perception's place
> But hardly co-exist in any case,
> Being its mere presentment—of the whole
> By parts, the simultaneous and the sole
> By the successive and the many.
>
> [II. 570–579; 487–595]

These words serve as fair warning to any student who wishes to hold Browning accountable for his metaphysical language. Words can only approximate a representation of one's perceptions, insists

---

7. Quoted in David Loth, *The Brownings: A Victorian Idyll,* p. 47.

Browning. Paracelsus learned that he could not know all; *Sordello* proves that one cannot express all, even the little that he knows. The esoteric metaphysical flights of the final section of the poem, inexcusably obscure though they still seem, one hundred thirty years following their publication, at least confirm Browning's lifelong conviction that "words are wild and weak."

As in *Paracelsus,* several of the references to God in *Sordello* are conventional or figurative:

> Plucker of amaranths grown beneath God's eye
> In gracious twilights where his chosen lie.
>
> [I. 371–372]

> Only obliged to ask himself, "What was,"
> A speedy answer followed; but, alas,
> One of God's large ones tardy to condense
> Itself into a period.
>
> [II. 721–724]

Missing in *Sordello,* however, is Paracelsus's propensity for equating God's will with his own. Although Sordello faces crises as intense as those of the equally egocentric Parcelsus, he knows his limitations and accepts the reality of a higher power not subject to his feelings. In fact, Power is exactly Sordello's definition of God. Festus's God as Love, Aprile's God as Poet, and Paracelsus's God as Mind have become Sordello's God as Power or Will. Twenty-four times the poem mentions *Will* as a noun, sometimes appearing to refer to human, sometimes divine, power:

> The Body, the Machine for Acting Will,
> Had been at the commencement proved unfit;
> That for Demonstrating, Reflecting it,
> Mankind—no fitter: was the Will Itself
> In fault?
>
> [II. 994–998]

> Nought is Alien in the world—my Will
> Own all already; yet can turn it—still
> Less—Native, since my Means to correspond
> With Will are so unworthy.
>
> [III. 175–178]

Whether Will has transcendental or human connotations, its significance lies in its relation to the human soul. Browning's preoccupation with the development of the soul—in spite of the crowded background of historical data which detract from the poem's primary concern at times—is perhaps the only indisputable fact about the poem. *Sordello* traces a life in some respects quite like Paracelsus. He would become "Monarch of the World!"

> Never again
> Sordello could in his own sight remain
> One of the many, one with hopes and cares
> And interest nowise distinct from their . . .
> The divorce
> Is clear: why needs Sordello square his course
> By any known example?"
>
> [II. 367–370; 377–379]

Like Paracelsus also, he uses his peers to lead him to further knowledge of himself:

> While our Sordello only cared to know
> About men as a means whereby he'd show
> Himself, and men had much or little worth
> According as they kept in or drew forth
> That self.
>
> [IV. 620–624]

There are similarities. The conflicts of imagination and experience, isolation and communication, pure will and external exigencies, and perception and articulation to be met in *Sordello* are stated in one form or another in the earlier poem. They are all important to the development of the soul.

Sordello's basic approach to life's major problems illustrates the soul's primacy. He trusts his feelings to lead him to the truth: "I feel, am what I feel, know what I feel; / So much is truth to me." But accompanying this consciousness of the individual's pre-eminence is a corresponding realization of his limitations:

> For thus
> I bring Sordello to the rapturous
> Exclaim at the crowd's cry, because one round
> Of life was quite accomplished; and he found
> Not only that a soul, whate'er its might,

Is insufficient to its own delight,
Both in corporeal organs and in skill
By means of such to body forth its Will.

[III. 561–568]

Sordello learns, much more rapidly than Paracelsus, that to be human is to be a creature as well as a creator. To be a man is to know that one cannot be God. Struggle, temptation, frustration, conflict—these are the marks of man. But through them he can find salvation, provided he focus his life on a high calling, "a progress thus pursued / Through all existence." His obstacles can become stepping stones to rise above his limitations:

Whereas for Mankind springs
Salvation by each hindrance interposed.
They climb; life's view is not at once disclosed
Heaven plain above them, yet of wings bereft:
But lower laid, as at the mountain's foot.

[VI. 274–279]

To accomplish all its goals, overcome all obstacles, and thus test and prove itself through trial, the soul has one more need: to escape the boundaries of time.

To be complete for, satisfy the whole
Series of spheres—Eternity, his soul
Needs must exceed, prove incomplete for, each
Single sphere—Time.

[VI. 551–554]

Sordello needs time beyond death to finish his course. From his recognition of his weakness and imperfection, his finitude, springs a conviction and a hope of life beyond death.

This discussion has been about the soul and not about God. *Sordello* is not, in any usual sense, a religious poem. For most of its 5800 lines, God receives little consideration. His subordination to the soul, however, does not diminish His awesome majesty. In the soul's preoccupation with itself, he discovers his ontological need for a power beyond and above himself:

Ah, my Sordello, I this once befriend
And speak for you. Of a Power above you still
Which, utterly incomprehensible,

54

Is out of rivalry, which thus you can
Love, tho' unloving all conceived by man—
What need! And of—none the minutest duct
To that out-nature, nought that would instruct
And so let rivalry begin to live—
But of a Power its representative
Who, being for authority the same,
Communication different, should claim
A course, the first chose but this last revealed—
This Human clear, as that Divine concealed—
What utter need!

[VI. 590–603]

From the depths of the soul grows the consciousness of a supreme power and a desire for its concrete revelation in human form. Here, rather than in historical proof or scientific evidence, is found Browning's only trusted evidence for God. It is a familiar argument: God exists because man's being demands his existence. The need stated to Sordello here becomes in later poems Browning's answer in faith to the growing host of Victorian skeptics who would dismiss God as unknowable and irrelevant to man. For Browning, man's greatness demands God's grandeur.

Thus Sordello's exploration of faith corroborates the conclusions drawn from Browning's earlier poems. In these poems, Browning always begins his investigation of religious faith existentially, asserting the supremacy of the individual soul who confronts his destiny alone and can rely upon no external power as final authority over his life. Having only his mind, senses, and intuitions to guide him, he then submits his subjective convictions to experimentation in an objective world, using that world (and persons within—and above—it) to measure and reflect those convictions, and to help him chart the furthermost limitations of his ability. He repeatedly underscores the psychological necessity for a goal-orientated life to provide organization, hope, and ultimate salvation for the soul. That future toward which man looks must be ever before him, even at the grave. From man's incompleteness, Browning argues for additional time to perfect himself. Finally, Browning reiterates his doctrine that the soul's limitations and its intuitions of an inexplicable but nonetheless actual transcendent reality must be expressed. Although language cannot define or account for this reality, it is nonetheless employed to approximate the soul's apprehension of the reality. To speak of

God as Love or Mind or Poet or Power or Will is not to delimit God's nature; words cannot capture the incomprehensible. They can only point to something beyond themselves.

Each of these four elements of Browning's faith will be more fully explored in the three following chapters. They form the basis for his experiments in faith in the religious dramatic monologues.

The Existential Posture

Robert Browning, the respectable Victorian man about town, elegant in attire, eloquent in conversation, and everywhere in demand in the finest circles, was in but not of his society. The picture of the dashing young socialite, or of the gallant Saint George rescuing his middle-aged Lady from her wicked dragon-father, or of the aging gentleman proud that he looked more like a banker than a poet and quite happy to be idolized by fervent disciples, is not the total picture of Browning. After the parties, away from the noise of countless conversations on innumerable current topics (including, it seems almost everything but poetry and religion), Browning returned to the quietness of his meditations, brooding over what really mattered to him, mattered so much that he did not care to vulgarize or endanger his ideas by submitting them to those who would misunderstand them or dispute them. Believing God to be above the grasp of dialectic and reason, and faith to be a matter of action and not disputation, he preferred to explore the implications and possible contradictions of his personal religion in the depths of his soul, sharing them poetically but not socially. Comfortable in the superficialities of Victorian society but ill at ease in its intellectual world, Browning could find no spiritual companionship among its academic or religious institutions. Both the artificial rigors of universities and the arbitrary dogmas of churches offended him; he found no authoritative voice to answer his soul's most imperative questions. He was too intelligent to be satisfied with the obvious or traditional and too independent to trust himself unquestioningly to any book or institution. He could only look to his own resources for his answers. He summarized the intellectual loneliness of his whole career (except for his genuine fellowship with Elizabeth Barrett) when he wrote to Miss Isa Blagden in 1865, "As I began, so shall I end—taking my own course, pleasing myself or aiming at doing so, and thereby, I hope, pleasing God."[1] He had earlier expressed the same sentiment to another friend, Julia Wedgwood: "I live more and more . . . for God, not man—I don't care what men think now, knowing they will never think my thoughts, yet I need increasingly to tell *the truth*."[2] Browning's intellectual and spiritual alienation from his fellow men, his refusal to trust anyone else in religious issues, his rejection of systematic philosophies and theologies, and his fiercely individualistic and subjective faith, place him in the company of several existentialists discussed in the first chapter.

Browning's existential posture is reflected in every religious poem. His characters are men alone. Alienated from common humanity, distinct from the natural world, sensing but unable to explain a spiritual reality, and feeling all too concretely their limitations, they learn the meaning of their solitude. Although Browning presents a few characters who radiate optimism (Rabbi Ben Ezra, Abt Vogler, and Pippa), most of Browning's men and women are alienated, bewildered human beings. Searching for happiness in hopeful struggle, they are seldom shown realizing that hope. Although they may be surrounded with other people, their religious struggles cannot be shared; in fact, the presence of others only intensifies their loneliness. Missing in all of Browning's writings is any sense of the group, of community. The title of one work is *Men and Women,* but it is a collection of individual poems about individual persons who enjoy little interaction. Browning expresses no concern for humanity in general, only for individuals. His men seldom fight for the great principles which have alleviated human suffering or intellectual darkness. Browning is concerned about a man, not about man. He failed as a playwright, H. B. Charlton believes, because of this intensely individual outlook: Browning "looked out on life and saw it as an aggregation of separate human souls seeking their relation to God. He never saw, never felt the real existence of the something or other besides God and yet not ourselves which gives its vital force to a community."[3] Drama,

1. Browning to Isabella Blagden, from Ste.-Marie, August 19, 1865. *Dearest Isa: Robert Browning's Letters to Isabella Blagden,* edited by Edward C. McAleer, p. 220.

2. Browning to Julia Wedgwood, July 28, 1864. *Robert Browning and Julia Wedgwood: A Broken Friendship as Revealed by Their Letters,* edited by Richard Curle, pp. 33–34.

3. "Browning as Dramatist," *Bulletin of The John Rylands* Library XXIII, p. 45.

a corporate activity, builds on interrelationships among people. At least in religious matters, Browning was not concerned with such relationships. A man confronts God personally, existentially, the poet believed. The only reliable information upon which religious decisions can be made is personal. Ultimate truth cannot be pressed into verbal propositions or safeguarded by hallowed institutions. The final authority in religious choice is the chooser. In his uncertainty and loneliness, Browning's man must choose for himself what he will become. Choosing to believe in God, desiring to satisfy Him, he admits that it is belief and not knowledge which motivates him.

In 1850, four years after his marriage to Elizabeth Barrett, Robert Browning published *Christmas-Eve and Easter-Day,* one of his most explicit religious statements. The fruit of half a lifetime's contemplation and of marriage to an intensely religious woman, the poem fulfills a promise he made to her in the days of their courtship: "You speak out, *you,*—I only make men and women speak—give you truth broken into prismatic hues, and fear the pure white light, even if it is in me, but I am going to try."[4] The result is a poem which reveals similarities to Miss Barrett's religious thinking, but the basic approach to questions of faith is in the familiar Browning style.

It is generally believed that his marriage to Elizabeth Barrett led Browning to expose his religious convictions in this important poem. Without a doubt, *Christmas-Eve and Easter-Day* does reflect the tone and conclusions of their correspondence several years earlier, a correspondence as noteworthy in its unexpected minimum of discussion about religion as for their discovery of a mutual religious outlook.[5] Several months after they had begun writing, after she had been

---

4. Browning to Elizabeth Barrett, January 13, 1845. *The Letters of Robert Browning and Elizabeth Barrett Browning,* edited by Robert Barrett Browning, I, 6.

5. It should be noted that Miss Barrett's letters to her several friends demonstrate her genuine enthusiasm for religious discussions, as does her later study of spiritualism. Browning's letters, on the other hand, evidence the same reticence on such issues as records of his polite social conversations reveal. When writing to women, he frequently demonstrates his affection for them with a conventional "God bless you" or "if God please help us." These conventions are sprinkled throughout his writing to Miss Barrett, and later to Miss Isa Blagden. But when writing to his men friends—like William Story—or in his general correspondence, such terms are highly infrequent. In all his letters, genuine personal religious testimony is absent. Even in writing to Miss Barrett, he discusses religious topics in response to her probing or confessing. He does not initiate them, and when responding to her initiatives, he seldom moves beyond response to confession.

assured of Robert's affection, Miss Barrett confessed both her liberal understanding of Christianity and her Dissenting heritage:

> And talking of Italy and the cardinals, and thinking of some cardinal points you are ignorant of, did you ever hear that I was one of
>
> "those schismatiques
> Of Amsterdam"
>
> whom your Dr. Donne would have put into the dykes? unless he meant the Baptists, instead of the Independents, the holders of the Independent church principle. No—not "schismatical," I hope, hating as I do from the roots of my heart all that rending of the garment of Christ, which Christians are so apt to make the daily week-day of this Christianity so-called—and caring very little for most dogmas and doxies in themselves—too little, as people say to me sometimes, (when they send me "New Testaments" to learn from, with very kind intentions)—and be- lieving that there is only one church in heaven and earth, with one divine High Priest to it; let exclusive religionists build what walls they please and bring out what chrisms. But I used to go with my father always, when I was able, to the nearest dissent- ing chapel of the Congregationalists—from liking the simplicity of that praying and speaking without books—and a little too from disliking the theory of state churches. There is a narrow- ness among the dissenters which is wonderful; an arid, grey Puritanism in the clefts of their souls; but it seems to me clear that they know what the "liberty of Christ" means, far better than those do who call themselves "churchmen"; and stand al- together, as a body, on higher ground.[6]

Robert Browning's reply assures her of the similarity of their beliefs:

> Can it be you, my own you past putting away, you are a schis- matic and frequenter of Independent Dissenting Chapels? And you confess to *me*—whose father and mother went this morning to the very Independent Chapel where they took me, all those years back, to be baptized—and where they heard, this morn- ing, a sermon preached by the very minister who officiated on that other occasion![7]

6. Elizabeth Barrett to Browning, August 2, 1845. *Letters*, I, 145–146.
7. Browning to Elizabeth Barrett, August 4, 1845. *Letters*, I, 147–148.

Thus, early in their remarkable love affair, the two poets discovered their religious affinity. Both were brought up as Dissenters, both were conversant with the scriptures and the values of Christianity—and both were impatient with doctrinal or ecclesiastical narrowness and reserved the right to select their own forms of worship. Mrs. Browning later admitted to her friend Leigh Hunt that, while she believed in the divinity of Jesus Christ ("in the intensest sense—that he was God absolutely"), she was on all other issues "very unorthodox," finding all churches in her time as "too narrow and low to hold true Christianity in its proximate developments."[8] A few years earlier, she had written her brother to refute, to him, at least, charges against her that she was tending toward Unitarianism. She reaffirmed her faith: "If a union with the Christian church means a recognition of Jesus Christ as my Lord and my God, then it is a calumnious error to represent me as a schismatic from the church and an example of modern infidelity."[9]

Miss Barrett's outspoken professions of her faith have led critics to conclude that in addition to her general influence on Robert Browning, she was specifically responsible for both the undertaking and the content of *Christmas-Eve and Easter-Day*. It is a fact that scholars can point to one of her letters, written nearly a year later than her first confession of faith to Browning, which contains nearly all the elements of the poem:

> Dearest, when I told you yesterday, after speaking of the many coloured theologies of the house, that it was hard to answer for what *I* was . . . I meant that I felt unwilling, for my own part, to put on any of the liveries of the sects. The truth, as God sees it, must be something so different from these opinions about truth—these systems which fit different classes of men like their coats, and wear brown at the elbows always. I believe in what is divine and floats at highest, in all these different theologies—and because the really Divine draws together souls, and tends so to a unity, I could pray anywhere and with all sorts of worshippers, from the Sistine Chapel to Mr. Fox's, those kneeling and those standing. Wherever you go, in all religious societies, there is a

8. Note appended to R. Browning's letter of October 6, 1857. *Letters of Robert Browning Collected by Thomas J. Wise,* edited by Thurman L. Hood, p. 50.

9. Elizabeth Barrett to George Barrett, January 10, 1854. *Letters of the Brownings to George Barrett,* edited by Paul Landis with Ronald E. Freeman, p. 208.

little to revolt, and a good deal to bear with—but it is not otherwise in the world without; and, *within,* you are especially reminded
that God has to be more patient than yourself after all. Still you go
quickest there, where your sympathies are least ruffled and dis-
turbed—and I like, beyond comparison best, the simplicity of the
dissenters . . . Well—there is enough to dissent from among the
dissenters—the Formula is rampant among them as among
others—you hear things like the buzzing of flies in proof of a
corruption—and see every now and then something divine set
up like a post for men of irritable minds and passions to rub
themselves against, calling it a holy deed—you feel moreover
bigotry and ignorance pressing on you on all sides, till you gasp
for breath like one strangled. But better this, even, than what
is elsewhere . . . The Unitarians seem to me to throw over what
is most beautiful in the Christian Doctrine; but the Formulists,
on the other side, stir up a dust, in which appears excusable
not to see. When the veil of the body falls, how we shall look
into each other's faces, astonished . . . after one glance at
God's![10]

Again Browning's reply shows his agreement and enthusiasm:
"Dearest, I know your very meaning, in what you said of religion,
and responded to it with my whole soul—what you express now,
is for us both."[11] When Miss Barrett's letter is placed beside Browning's
poem, his indebtedness to her for the specific treatment of the Dissenter's Chapel, the Roman Catholic basilica, and even the rationalistic

10. Elizabeth Barrett to R. Browning, August 15, 1846. *Letters,* II, 429–430.
11. Browning to Elizabeth Barrett, August 17, 1846. *Letters,* II, 436. He continues:
"Those are my own feelings, my convictions beside—instinct confirmed by reason.
Look at that injunction to 'love God with all the heart, and soul, and strength'—and
then imagine yourself bidding any faculty, that arises towards the love of him, be
still! If in a meeting house, with the blank white walls, and a simple doctrinal
exposition,—all the senses should turn (from where they lie neglected) to all that
sunshine in the Sistine with its music and painting, which would lift them at once
to Heaven,—why should you not go forth?—to return just as quickly, when they are
nourished into a luxuriance that extinguishes, what is called, Reason's pale wavering
light, lamp or whatever it is—for I have got into a confusion with thinking of our
convolvuluses that climb and tangle round the rose-trees—which might be lamps or
tapers! See the levity! No—this sort of levity only exists because of the strong conviction,
I do believe! There seems no longer need of earnestness in assertion, or proof . . . so
it runs lightly over, like foam on the top of a wave."

lecture, seems clear. Equally clear is their agreement that the "truth, as God sees it," must differ from the many opinions about it. What is not proved by the comparison is that Browning's religious opinions were derivatives of Miss Barrett's, as some of his critics would like to contend.

When the poem is read immediately following *Pauline* and *Paracelsus,* poems as much concerned with religious truth as *Christmas-Eve and Easter-Day,* the reader can see that Browning's fundamental religious orientation has not changed at all. Of course, *Christmas-Eve and Easter-Day* is more topical, more relevant to contemporary problems, and more obviously Browning's own statement than the earlier poems. The speakers are no longer quite like the Promethean Paracelsus, straining against the chains binding him in his humanity. The struggle occurs below the mythological scale. The speakers are, if not Browning, then persons very much like him—and very much like *Pauline*'s poet and like Paracelsus approaching his death. Questions of doubt and certainty, of faith and knowledge, of mind and heart, of time and eternity—questions pervading the early poems, are in this one. The focus—in spite of all the interest in eternal forms of worship—remains upon the individual soul's relation to God. As isolated from his peers as Paracelsus was from his, each speaker in the two parts of this poem is cut off from a genuine religious context. He is man alone, seeking God.

In *Christmas-Eve* the attention devoted to the three methods of observing Christ's birth does not obscure the loneliness of the speaker. As a fully mature individual, he has grown away from belief in the doctrines and simple rituals of his Dissenter upbringing. When he returns to worship in his former way, cold stares and contemptuous regard greet him, reflecting his own withdrawal from the fellowship of these worshippers. Although within their building, he is no longer one of them. He cannot share their simple prejudiced piety. He is alone. When taken in his vision to St. Peter's, he views the majestic building from a solitary vantage point. From outside, his vision pierces through the wall into the bustling activity of the worship service at the moment of the Holy Sacrament. But he is still alone, "left outside the door." In the vision of the Göttingen lecture hall, "ranged decent and symmetrical," he learns of a demythologized Jesus, stripped of his mystery and sovereignty, duly explained and categorized through the ratiocinations of arid scholarship. Jesus Christ, Son of God, has become "a right true man,"

Whose work was worthy a man's endeavor:
Work, that gave warrant almost sufficient
                    To his disciples, for rather believing
He was just omnipotent and omniscient.

[878–882]

The speaker listens politely but unsympathetically, leaving at his first opportunity—to be again, as he was before, alone. When he returns from his visions to the chapel scene, his nearest neighbor confirms his isolation: "She had slid away a contemptuous space."

He is not only isolated from other human beings; to his social loneliness is added cosmic loneliness. Never really questioning the existence of God,[12] he nonetheless experiences God's qualitative and spatial distance from him:

You know what I mean: God's all, man's nought:
But also, God, whose pleasure brought
Man into being, stands away
                    As it were a handbreath off, to give
Room for the newly-made to live.

[288–292]

Acknowledging God's supremacy, but having to live "as though no God there were,"[13] the man must assert himself to free the power within him. His worship of God stems from his impotence compared with God; unsuccessful in finding the one true worship, he can only return to his true concern, speaking of and for himself only:

Meantime, I can but testify
God's care for me—no more, can I—
It is but for myself I know.

[1185–1187]

and even that knowledge admits no proof:

Have I been sure, this Christmas-Eve,
God's own hand did the rainbow weave,
Whereby the truth from heaven slid
Into my soul?

[1203–1206]

12. See lines 279 f.
13. *Paracelsus*, I, 188.

No irrefutable answer can be given; only a profession of faith: "I only knew he named my name." His review of the Dissenter, Roman Catholic, and Unitarian-Liberal-Rationalistic understandings of the Incarnation demonstrated the ugliness, arrogance, and exclusiveness of all of them—but yielded no reasons for changing from his flawed but familiar Dissenting tradition. Hence, "I choose here!" His only stated reason for the choice, the thinner "human veil" which the Chapel places between worshipper and God, is more a testimony to his upbringing than to any objective weighing of the alternatives. No claim is made for the Chapel's strict adherence to the scriptures, the usual Protestant boast. In fact, the contrary claim is made:

> The zeal was good, and the aspiration;
> And yet, and yet, yet, fifty times over,
> Pharaoh received no demonstration,
> By his Baker's dream of Baskets Three,
> Of the doctrine of the Trinity.
>
> [230–234]

No argument is presented for its authority as the divinely established church of Christ. As a matter of fact, in this survey of religious forms, Browning does not once raise the question of the ultimate claims of any of these branches of Christianity upon him as the authoritative representatives of God's will on earth. There is no hint here of a Calvinistic belief, for example, in man's utter helplessness before an almighty and arbitrary God. Neither is there any hint of a Roman Catholic's dread of the Church's power of excommunicating for heresy (which heresy would include any implicit recognition of schismatic bodies as legitimate members of the Christian church). Browning's Christian is a man isolated from human fellowship and distant from God, but he is the free sovereign of his life: he chooses his own worship because he believes it his right to do so.

The resemblance between the speaker's position and Browning's earlier similar statements to Elizabeth Barrett is too close to go unmentioned. In 1845, he expressed his belief in "private judgment," in moral struggle, and in "duty to yourself," which he equated with duty to God:

> I will tell you: all passive obedience and implicit submission of will and intellect is by far too easy, if well considered, to be the course prescribed by God to Man in this life of probation—for they *evade* probation altogether, though foolish people think

otherwise . . . But there is no reward proposed for the feat of breathing, and a great one for that of believing—consequently there must go a great deal more of voluntary effort to this latter than is implied in the getting absolutely rid of it at once, by adopting the direction of an infallible church, or private judgment of another—for all our life is some form of religion, and all our action some belief, and there is but one law, however modified, for the greater and the less. In your case I do think you are called upon to do your duty to yourself; that is, to God in the end.[14]

Browning's letter and the poem's speaker prove that, for them, the religious choice is not a rational one. When the speaker hears the German professor's lecture, he rejects not only his conclusions but also his rationalistic premise, which makes the human mind the measure of all things and places all confidence in scientific logic. There is more to man than mind. Preaching, arguing, debating, lecturing—all such methods are effective only with those who already believe what they are trying to prove:

> The same endeavour to make you believe,
> And with much the same effect, no more:
>   Each method abundantly convincing,
> As I say, to those convinced before,
>   But scarce to be swallowed without wincing
> By the not-as-yet-convinced.

[266–271]

Because he places the foundation of faith elsewhere than the mind, the speaker appreciates that the Dissenters, so ill instructed by their ignorant preacher, can know what the narrowly rationalistic German professor can never know:

> These people have really felt, no doubt,
> A something, the motion they style the Call of them;
>   And this is their method of bringing about,
> By a mechanism of words and tones,
> (So many tests in so many groans)
> A sort of reviving and reproducing,
>   More or less perfectly, (who can tell?)

14. *Letters,* I, 220–221.

The mood itself, which strengthens by using;
And how that happens, I understand well.

[240–248]

He illustrates his understanding by a homely example:

A tune was born in my head last week,
Out of the thump-thump and shriek-shriek
　　Of the train, as I came by it, up from Manchester;
And when, next week, I take it back again,
My head will sing to the engine's clack again,
　　While it only makes my neighbour's haunches stir,
—Finding no dormant musical sprout
In him, as in me, to be jolted out.

[249–256]

The incommunicability of the tune makes it no less real. Defying any efforts to verbalize it, the tune elicits the private joy of the speaker. He will recall it whenever he hears the train's rumblings. This, then, is the value of worship and teaching and preaching: unable to persuade anyone to new truths, it can nevertheless recall and reinforce past experiences.

'T is the taught already that profits by teaching;
He gets no more from the railway's preaching
　　Than, from this preacher who does the rail's office, I;
Whom therefore the flock cast a jealous eye on.

[257–261]

Congregational worship depends upon common experiences and backgrounds to bind people together. Those individuals who, because of different social or economic or national or racial or educational backgrounds, do not share such experiences, cannot readily have fellowship with those who do. Browning suggests a kind of sociological determinism which partially accounts for the loneliness of the speaker. His individual experiences have made him not quite like any other worshippers; his background has alienated him from them. Through his travels and his reading he has learned the relativity of worship and can no longer be persuaded by sermons or rituals or lectures to accept a narrow, partisan church. Able to view each Christmas-Eve service with the objectivity of an outsider, he is unable to commune with any of the insiders. When he does return to the Chapel from

67

his visionary excursion, he finds himself within the building but not one of the fellowship.

The speaker's faith, in spite of his Dissenter education, rests on two evidences: nature and his own feelings.

> —In youth I looked to these very skies,
> And probing their immensities,
> I found God there, his visible power;
>> Yet felt in my heart, amid all its sense
>> Of the power, an equal evidence
> That his love, there too, was the nobler dower.

[279–284]

The evidence in nature of God's power is important, but secondary. His heart's feelings in effect state the *a priori* qualification of divinity. In this impulsive statement is the essence of Browning's faith: trusting the impulses of the heart above any other criterion, we must assert the divinity of love! The God he finds in nature is power—immense and awe-inspiring. But the heart's need is for love. Since the greatest human need is love, then the highest possible concept for God is love. Browning's highly-charged understanding of love then becomes the object of his worship, to which he attaches the name God. Reversing the Biblical statement, Browning here and throughout this poem confesses his faith that Love is God.

The stress on love solves a problem for the reader of *Christmas-Eve*. One would not ordinarily expect a poem about a man's search for the true form of worship to be written ironically, with the speaker detached and aloof from all of the presented options. The ironic attitude and the religious attitude are contradictory. If one's faith is his ultimate concern, he can never enjoy an ironic distance from its object. Yet the descriptions of the chapel, the basilica, and the lecture hall quite crudely burlesque their subjects. The problem of the use of irony is solved when one sees that the poem is not a search for a true form of worship or a deeper understanding of God at all. The visits to the worship houses provide the structure, and the confrontations with Christ move the speaker from place to place. But there is no real development of the speaker, no crisis for him. In fact, the poem is remarkable for its lack of genuine tension. The contrast between it and the agonized introspection of John Donne or Gerard Manley Hopkins is striking. What appears here to be a dramatic quest for religious meaning is really a didactic poem in dramatic form. The poet already knows what he believes and the

source of that belief. He believes in Love because his heart tells him
to. Having secured himself on a rock of Love, he can view from
above the religious controversy swirling beneath him.

Hence the speaker can easily assume a relativistic attitude towards
the various expressions of Christianity: they do not ultimately matter.
He can even accept the Roman Catholics, whose worship is so foreign
to his own:

> I see the error; but above
> The scope of error, see the love,—
> Oh, love of those first Christian days!
>
> [647–650]

Love enables the speaker to accept those whose form of worship
he finds offensive. When Christ appears to him, he recognizes him
as the embodiment of love:

> Thou art the love of God—above
> His power, didst hear me place his love,
> And that was leaving the world for thee.
>
> [459–461]

Christ has been stripped of all his other characteristics: teacher, healer,
miracle-worker, church-founder, Jewish Messiah. Like William Blake,
who appropriated Christ as a symbol for Higher Innocence in his
esoteric system, Browning has appropriated Christ to symbolize love
as the highest of human values, with no concern for historical accuracy.
This fusion of God-Christ and Love is made explicit in one passage:

> No: love which, on earth, amid all the shows of it,
>> Has ever been seen the sole good of life in it,
> The love, ever growing there, spite of the strife in it,
>> Shall arise, made perfect, from death's repose of it.
> And I shall behold thee, face to face,
> O God, and in thy light retrace
> How in all I loved here, still wast thou!
>
> [359–365]

Love is all for him: "the sole good of life," the means through which
his soul will continue to grow and develop, his assurance of life beyond
death. His way changes the meaning of worship from its traditional
service of God to an emphasis upon God's service to man. Even the
crucifixion is important, not for what it reveals about God, but for
what it reveals about love:

Does the precept run "Believe in good,
In justice, truth, now understood
For the first time?—or, "Believe in me,
Who lived and died, yet essentially
Am Lord of Life?" Whoever can take
The same to his heart and for mere love's sake
Conceive of the love,—that man obtains
A new truth.

[1052–1061]

The poet can speak confidently of the divinity of love because the evidence of the inner man supports this belief. The one reliable testimony to truth comes from within:

"Take all in a word: the truth in God's breast
Lies trace for trace upon ours impressed."

[1018–1019]

A man can be certain that he knows more in his conscience

Of what right is, than arrives at birth
    In the best man's acts that we bow before:
This last knows better—true, but my fact is,
'T is one thing to know, and another to practice.
And thence I conclude that the real God-function
Is to furnish a motive and injunction
For practising what we know already.

[1036–1042]

The speaker then finds that motive and injunction in Christ. His moral preoccupation (the same concern that is evident in his elevation of Love) informs this audacious passage, which clearly demonstrates his religious attitude. Having in several other lines noted the distance between man and God, he here claims that moral judgments can nonetheless confidently be made from within oneself, that the truth of the conscience is identical with the truth of God, that absolutes remain absolute although their names change, and finally that God's true function—an amazing word to use in a poem supposedly about God-worship—is to serve man's moral needs. Although the words connote the stable world of Platonic Ideas, the repeated insistence upon individual experience and intuition reminds the reader that for Browning, "Truth remains true, the fault's in the prover." He always posits absolutes when speaking metaphysically—but he consistently subordinates them to human considerations. The absolutes are posited because human development demands them; human beings do not grow toward Truth or Goodness because Truth and Goodness demand that growth. Browning insists upon beginning with human needs and desires, not with the demands of any Absolutes. On the other hand, any refusal to move beyond the human and relative to the fixed and unchanging is an invitation to personal sterility. He quarrels with each of the positions he examines in *Christmas-Eve* because they have fixed their attention upon temporary human forms rather than upon the truth those forms were meant to convey.

Two important images symbolize this approach. The first is the moon, presiding at times obscurely, once brilliantly, over the religious struggle below it. For Browning, the clouded moon represents man's normal condition, with man being unable to see the unobstructed truth. But at least he is generally vouchsafed a glimpse of it through a curtain of clouds. He can discern separately the colored components of the whiteness of truth, but seldom the white truth itself. Even in the one moment of the moon's full splendor, at Christ's coming in radiance, the speaker cannot see Christ's face—"only the sight of a sweepy garment, vast and white." He receives no full revelation of all metaphysical truth. What is revealed is Christ as the full embodiment of love, the highest example for human behavior. The speaker knows what he must do now: he must love. The obstructing forms of the clouds (like the obfuscating forms of the churches) can be swept away only by love. Truth, he realizes, is not something one knows; it is something one does. For Browning, as he proves in all his poems, love is usually concrete action, not an abstract principle. Without an unobstructed vision of truth, man can still act upon the limited truth that he does possess. He knows that he can love; therefore he must.

The second symbol reinforces the first. As the moon is vastly superior to the clouds which obscure it, so the living water of religious truth should not be replaced by a worship of the vessels which hold it:

> Shall I take on me to change his [God's] tasks,
> And dare, despatched to a river-head
>   For a simple draught of the element,
> Neglect the thing for which he sent,
>   And return with another thing instead?—

Saying, "Because the water found
Welling up from underground,
Is mingled with the taints of earth,
While thou, I know, dost laugh at dearth,
And couldst, at wink or word, convulse
The world with the leap of a river-pulse,—
Therefore I turned from the oozings muddy,
    And bring thee a chalice I found, instead:
See the brave veins in the breccia ruddy!
    One would suppose that the marble bled.
What matters the water? A hope I have nursed:
The waterless cup will quench my thirst."
—Better have knelt at the poorest stream
    That trickles in pain from the straitest rift!
    For the less or the more is all God's gift,
Who blocks up or breaks wide the granite-seam
And here, is there water or not to drink?

                                   [1279–1300]

Because all forms of worship are but vessels and of value only as they carry the living water, and because the Dissenter tradition places the least emphasis upon the vessel (or, as the speaker says in a switch of metaphor, placing "the thinnest human veil between"), he chooses, "in ignorance and weakness," to worship with the Dissenters:

    For the preachers's merit or demerit,
It were to be wished the flaws were fewer
    In the earthen vessel, holding treasure
Which lies as safe in a golden ewer;
    But the main thing is, does it hold good measure?
Heaven soon sets right all other matters!

                                     [1311–1316]

Christmas-Eve concludes with the singing of the doxology. From that note of confidence there is an abrupt shift in mood to the first words of *Easter-Day*: "How very hard it is to be / A Christian!" In the search for a correct form of worship—which was not a search at all but an exposé of the fallibility of all such forms—the speaker moved with assurance toward the pragmatic selection of the church of his childhood. *Easter-Day,* a dialogue between beliefs and doubts, explores genuine religious doubt and can end confidently only by removing the basis of faith from knowledge of God and his will to faith as an act of will. The believer is perplexed by the stringencies of Christian faith; the doubter questions both the credibility and the relevancy of Christianity. Christian practice, he claims, would be easy if Christian doctrines were only certain:

> Could I believe once thoroughly,
> The rest were simple. What? Am I
> An idiot, do you think—a beast?
> Prove to me, only that the least
> Command of God is God's indeed,
> And what injunction shall I need
> To pay obedience?
>
> [31–37]

But, as both believer and doubter admit, such proof of God's designs is inaccessible. Absolute knowledge of God cannot be ours. Far closer than our duty is our doubt:

> "I wish indeed 'God's kingdom come—'
> The day when I shall see appear
> His bidding, as my duty, clear
> From doubt!"
>
> [458–461]

The dialectic of the poem is complex: belief versus doubt, enjoyment versus rejection of this world's allures, faith as certainty versus faith as a leap, immortality versus oblivion beyond death. As usual with Browning, the dialectic leads nowhere. The believer can only appeal, finally, to personal experience. He recounts a remarkable vision in which he confronted Christ three years earlier. On a walk, meditating about life after death, he asks himself:

> "How were my case, now, did I fall
> Dead here, this minute—should I lie
> Faithful or faithless?"
>
> [396–398]

His answer comes in a vision of Judgment, a magnificent rending of the heavens which leaves

> exposed the utmost walls
> Of time, about to tumble in
> And end the world.
>
> [544–546]

It is an existential moment for him. He is alone, before the final Judge, choosing his destiny:

> There, stood I, found and fixed, I knew,
> Choosing the world. The choice was made;
> And naked and disguiseless stayed,
> And unevadable the fact.

[522–555]

From the voice out of eternity he learns that his desires have been granted. Having chosen to live for the pleasure of earth and not of the spirit, he would be granted the consequences of his choice. As a result, he would be forever shut out of the spiritual heaven.

In the joy of this verdict, he turns to explore his world. As the speaker in *Christmas-Eve* surveys religious establishments, this speaker searches for an empirical basis for his way of life. He turns to nature, which, divorced from any supernatural order, offers no evidence of life's plan or direction. Art, to which he turns next, can record man's hopes, struggles, and limitations—but it cannot serve as a basis for faith. He then proclaims "mind is best," testing reason as a foundation for faith. But the mind depends upon unreliable physical senses, thus is itself inadequate. Finally, realizing the emptiness of the strictly physical and temporal, he cries out:

> "Behold, my spirit bleeds,
> Catches no more at broken reeds,—
> But lilies flower those reeds above:
> I let the world go, and take love!
> Love survives in me, albeit those
> I love be henceforth masks and shows,
> Not living men and women: still
> I mind how love repaired all ill,
> Cured wrong, soothed grief, made earth amends
> With parents, brothers, children, friends!
>
> I pray,—
> Leave to love, only!

[931–940; 950–951]

Having chosen love, the speaker, a solitary figure alone on an abyss of nonbeing, like the Arab who "staggers blind / O'er a new tract of death, calcined / To aches, silence, nothingness," is now ready to realize a relationship with Christ, in whose eyes "the whole God"

74

embraces him. Only in Love, in reaching outward and being touched by both the human and the divine, can life's meaning be found. What begins as existential anguish, with a solitary figure seeking order in chaos, leads—not to a sense of absurdity and meaninglessness in his personal universe—but to an assertion of himself and a commitment to cosmic and personal love:

> —Now take love! Well betide
> Thy tardy conscience! Haste to take
> The show of love for the name's sake,
> Remembering every moment Who,
> Beside creating thee unto
> These ends, and these for thee, was said
> To undergo death in thy stead
> In flesh like thine: so ran the tale.
> What doubt in thee could countervail
> Belief in it? Upon the ground
> "That in the story had been found
> Too much love! How could God love so?"
> He who in all his works below,
> Adapted to the needs of man,
> Made love the basis of the plan,—
> Did love, as was demonstrated:
> While man, who was so fit instead
> To hate, as every day gave proof,—
> Man thought man, for his kind's behoof,
> Both could and did invent that scheme
> Of perfect love.
>
> [968–988]

This use of *love,* like Aprile's in *Paracelsus,* connotes more than appears at first. Christ invites the poet to step out of his isolation into relation, explaining that God, in addition to creating the universe, also created its parts to relate to each other. The tie that binds all its power and beauty and individual members together is love, inseparable from power and beauty, and ultimately inseparable from the fully human and fully faithful life. Love's ultimate demonstration was in Christ's crucifixion. This kind of love, for which man's soul cries out, seems almost above his own powers, for he seems "so fit instead / To hate." Christ's credentials as object of worship were offered on the cross, where he performed the sacrificial act of love which men's hearts demand but scarcely can perform.

Throughout his career, Browning experiments with the multivalence of *love,* as he experiments with *God.* As a result, we cannot always be certain of his meaning in any given context. In the passage quoted above, *love* sounds very much like neoplatonic love, the motive which binds and forms everything. But in the context of *Christmas-Eve and Easter-Day,* Browning is not exploring any metaphysical or ontological concept of love. His starting place is man alone, not man integrally placed within a Platonic system or order. He knows something of power and beauty, but finds both insufficient to satisfy himself totally. He has examined nature and art and intelligence, and found them equally inadequate. His manner of adopting love as his highest good closely resembles that of a twentieth-century situationist, for whom all absolutes have dissolved, and who must rely solely upon himself to make necessary ethical decisions. The situationist bases his decision on a self-chosen principle. For him, as for Browning, that principle is love. This love is not so much an abstract and absolute principle as an active relationship into which a man chooses to enter, freely committing himself. Eschewing both legalism and antinomianism, the situationist respects the ethical norms of his society and heritage, and he calls upon them to enlighten him. But he will not be bound by them if love dictates another course. Love is supreme. In neoplatonic thought, the ordered universe implies that every being is within the order regardless of his disposition. Browning, on the other hand, allots man a greater freedom and mobility; he can reject order. Thus he can experience what later popular existentialist writers call despair (*Angst*), as the speaker cries, "leave me not tied / To this despair." The threat of nonbeing and its corresponding anguish, dread, and isolation are real. His choice of love represents his determination to affirm meaning in his life and his universe. Even following his choice, there is no real assurance. In Paul Tillich's terms, he must exercise the "courage to be," subsuming doubt within his belief, because conclusive proof is missing. The speaker cannot even be certain of his moment of confrontation with Christ: "Was this a vision? False or true?" His final words suggest the ambiguity of his experience and the ambivalence of his response: "Mercy every way / Is infinite,— and who can say?"

Living as he must in uncertainty, his life remains a struggle. Earthly existence is a probationary period through which he labors toward future understanding:

Let me not know that all is lost,
Though lost it be—leave me not tied
To this despair, this corpse-like bride!
Let that old life seem mine—no more—
With limitation as before,
With darkness, hunger, toil, distress:
Be all the earth a wilderness!
Only let me go on, go on,
Still hoping ever and anon
To reach one eve the Better Land!

[994–1003]

Finally, accepting human and temporal limitations, he no longer demands absolute knowledge or total fulfillment upon earth. He prefers hope—even doubt—to knowledge, and struggle to tranquility. His warfare is not now against the human condition, but within it. He has gained the courage to be a man.

One further consideration remains. The importance of the Christ-figure to the movement of both *Christmas-Eve* and *Easter-Day* raises again the question of Browning's conception of the Incarnation. The answer is that the Christ of these poems, who appears to the speakers in majestic splendor, remains in both of them a nebulous symbol rather than a recognizable historical personality. He is Browning's creation. In *Christmas-Eve,* although he appears "with his human air," the speaker sees "the back of him, no more." He recognizes the hem of his "vast and white" garment; he is terrified. And when the figure turns toward him in blinding brightness, the speaker prostrates himself. In the journeys to Rome and Germany, he clasps only the hem of the garment, and this awesome Christ is called the "love of God." In *Easter-Day,* Christ appears as Judge, meeting the speaker in his vision of death. The description is more vivid than in *Christmas-Eve,* but Christ is no more real:

He stood there. Like the smoke
Pillared o'er Sodom, when day broke,—
I saw Him. One magnific pall
Mantled in massive fold and fall
His head, and coiled in snaky swathes
About His feet: night's black, that bathes
All else, broke, grizzled with despair,
Against the soul of blackness there.

[640–647]

The awfulness of the moment reduces the speaker to a mass, "no more now." The unmoving Judge pronounces his verdict upon the repentent believer, allows him to re-enter the struggle of life toward heaven, and reveals himself to him. The speaker calls him "Thou Love of God!" Hearing this supplication,

> Then did the form expand, expand—
> I knew Him through the dread disguise
> As the whole God within His eyes
> Embraced me.

> [1004–1007]

These descriptions of Christ are all we learn directly of him in a long two-part poem supposedly about his birth and resurrection—the two most significant events in his life and in Christian history. But the historical consequences of these events are irrelevant to Browning, as is the nineteenth-century preoccupation with their historicity. Missing also is any concern with theological considerations: Jesus of Nazareth as the expected Jewish Messiah; Christ's earthly ministry of teaching, healing, miracle-working; the traditional meaning of the incarnation as the earthly embodiment of God; the Atonement as a substitutionary sacrifice; the Church as the divinely instituted Body of Christ. The Christ of these poems is not the Christ of orthodox Christianity. He is rather the archetypal Love, the incarnation—not of God—but of Browning's mature and complex conception of Love. In spite of Browning's treatment of the German professor's rejection of the historical aspects of Christ's story, Browning himself has simply lifted Christ out of his scriptural context and transformed him to his purposes, emphasizing his role as the incarnation of love but ignoring or de-emphasizing every other aspect of his biography. As in his earlier poems, Browning's religious statements begin with man's needs and desires and move outward to find their satisfaction. Browning's Christ offers this satisfaction. He appears to men in moments of decision, in concrete events in real lives. He illustrates Browning's existential belief in love.

Turning from *Christmas-Eve and Easter-Day,* published in 1850, to *Saul,* published in final form five years later, we find an ideal companion piece for the 1850 poem. Shorter and more direct, *Saul* has always been one of Browning's most popular poems, perhaps for the wrong reasons. The Pre-Raphaelites admired its lush language, the Rhymers' Club its poetic beauty, and the London Browning Society its uplifting moral and spiritual message. It contains all of these. What has not been sufficiently noted, perhaps, is its adoption of the same existential posture to be found in all Browning's other religious poems.

Claims for Miss Barrett's influence upon Browning's poem seem exaggerated, as were such claims for the earlier poem. In fact, critics seem altogether too quick to assume Browning's dependency upon Miss Barrett in both his poetic and his religious thinking.

Adopting a more dramatic and objective form than *Christmas-Eve and Easter-Day* through the use of historical characters, *Saul* nonetheless arrives at the same conclusions by the same methods. In the first place, *Saul* begins with human need. The lethargic king, benumbed by his guilt and burdens, unable or unwilling to eat and drink, has sent for the young shepherd boy to cheer him. David responds with every talent he possesses. He sings of the common joys of life; he appeals to the "wild joys of living," happily affirming "How good is man's life, the mere living!" He praises the king, upon whose head "all gifts, which the world offers singly," combine. Saul is partially aroused by these affirmations, but remains unhealed. David recognizes the temporary effectiveness of his appeals:

> "Yea, my King,"
> I began—"thou dost well in rejecting mere comforts
>   that spring
> From the mere mortal life held in common by man and
>   by brute:
> In our flesh grows the branch of this life, in our soul
>   it bears fruit."
>
> [147–150]

The merely physical cannot satisfy the spiritual demands of the human soul. Nor can the best efforts of other human beings. David is impotent to cure Saul. In David's desperate desire to assist his king, the poem's focus shifts from the passive Saul to the loving David, who in his struggle finds the meaning of faith.

From the need—Saul's for comfort and David's for a means to comfort—the poem moves toward fulfillment of the need. Reviewing in order the alternative possibilities (exactly as *Christmas-Eve and Easter-Day* reviews alternative forms of worship and bases for belief), David tries the physical and human, then turns toward spiritual considerations. His reasoning sounds like a page out of Descartes. The philosopher had reasoned from his ability to think of God to belief

in God. David reasons from his ability to love to belief in the love
of God, admitting that God must have given him such an impulse
to love:

> And oh, all my heart how I loved him! but where was
> the sign?
> I yearned—"Could I help thee, my father, inventing
> a bliss,
> I would add, to that life of the past, both the
> future and this;
> I would give thee new life altogether, as good,
> ages hence,
> As this moment,—had love but the warrant, love's
> heart to dispense!"

[232–236]

With his yearning comes also his vision of the finality of love ("All's
love, yet all's law."), the magnitude of God ("God is seen God / In
the star, in the stone, in the flesh, in the soul and the clod"), and
the corresponding incompleteness of man ("the submission of man's
nothing-perfect to God's all-complete"). But his desire in human weakness to love another proves to him that one stronger also loves:

> Do I find love so fully in my nature, God's ultimate
> gift,
> That I doubt his own love can compete with it? Here
> the parts shift?
> Here, the creature surpass the Creator,—the end,
> what Began?
> Would I fain in my impotent yearning do all for this man,
> And dare doubt he alone shall not help him, who yet
> alone can?
> Would it ever have entered my mind, the bare will, much
> less power,
> To bestow on this Saul what I sang of, the marvelous
> dower
> Of the life he was gifted and filled with? to make
> such a soul,
> Such a body, and then such an earth for insphering
> the whole?

And doth it not enter my mind (as my warm tears attest)
These good things being given, to go on, and give one
                    more, the best?
Ay, to save and redeem and restore him, maintain at the
                    height
This perfection,—succeed with life's dayspring, death's
                    minute of night?
Interpose at the difficult minute, snatch Saul the mistake,
Saul the failure, the ruin he seems now,—and bid him awake
From the dream, the probation, the prelude, to find himself set
Clear and safe in new light and new life,—a new harmony yet
To be run, and continued, and ended—who knows?—or endure!
The man taught enough, by life's dream, of the rest to
                    make sure;
By the pain-throb, triumphantly winning intensified bliss,
And the next world's reward and repose, by the struggles
                    in this.

                                        [266–286]

He reasons, then, from Saul's need to human desire and inability to fulfill the need, to One who must be able to perform what men can only desire. He correspondingly reasons from the boundaries of time to the endless moments of eternity. Out of his frustrations comes his conviction:

                    What stops my desire?
This;—'t is not what man Does which exalts him, but what
                    man Would do!

                                        [294–295]

Limited though they be, men achieve greatness in attempting great things.
   Nothing is greater than love. Man, being unable to love as fully as he would, looks to a God of love, a God who will make that love known. The poem moves from the suffering Saul, who needs love, to the attending David, who gives love, then finally to a vision of Perfect Love. David cannot help Saul ultimately, for love is active and more beneficial to the agent than to the recipient. Since David, and not Saul, is the lover, the poem's focus must shift from the suffering king to his servant, who, in the action of love, comprehends the meaning of life. Love is an act, not a principle. It is self-sacrifice. It is flesh and blood assisting others. Its perfect incarnation is Christ.

'T is the weakness in the strength, that I cry for!
my flesh, that I seek
In the Godhead! I seek and I find it. O Saul,
it shall be
A Face like my face that receives thee; a Man like to me,
Thou shalt love and be loved by, for ever: a Hand like
this hand
Shall throw open the gates of new life to thee! See
the Christ stand!

[308–312]

Again Browning has brought us to Christ as Love Incarnate. David's reverence for Christ expresses Browning's own, which he often spoke of in the words of Charles Lamb, "If Christ entered the room I should fall on my knees," or of Napoleon, "I am an understander of men, and He was no man."[15] He was Love.

The poem is unified by three images which function like the moon and clouds and the water and cup in *Christmas-Eve*. The first is the cross. In the fourth section we meet Saul on the cross:

He stood as erect as that tent-prop, both arms stretched
out wide
On the great cross-support in the centre, that goes to
each side.

[28–29]

This is a secular cross, prior to its sanctification by Christ. It is simply the place of suffering, of punishment for sin. Saul's suffering, unlike Christ's, is involuntary. David's assignment is immediately apparent: he must bring Saul down from the cross and keep him down, alleviating his suffering and assuaging his guilt. Through David's ministrations, Saul feels some relief. By section eight, he has moved his head; in ten, he stands; in fifteen, only one arm is around the tent prop, and then Saul sits. That is as far as David's help can take him. He cannot fully restore him. Human endeavor in behalf of another, like everything else human, is limited.

To make certain we understand this limitation, Browning employs his second major image in the tenth section:

15. Quoted in Orr, *Life and Letters,* pp. 462–463.

Then Saul, who hung propped
By the tent's cross-support in the centre, was struck
             by his name.
Have ye seen when Spring's arrowy summons goes right to
             the aim,
And some mountain, the last to withstand her,
             that held (he alone,
While the vale laughed in freedom and flowers)
             on a broad bust of stone
A year's snow bound about for a breastplace,—
             leaves grasp of the sheet?
Fold on fold all at once it crowds thunderously down
             to his feet,
And there fronts you, stark, black, but alive yet,
             your mountain of old,
With his rents, the successive bequeathings of ages untold—
Yes, each harm got in fighting your battles, each
             furrow and scar
Of his head thrust 'twixt you and the tempest—all hail,
             there they are!
—Now again to be softened with verdure, again hold the nest
Of the dove, tempt the goat and its young to the green
             on his crest
For their food in the ardours of summer.

                                        [102–115]

In a provocative reversal of Browning's customary use of light and
dark, he has the sun in the spring release the mountain from its
prison of snow. Now the mountain can be softened with verdure.
But it is still the same old mountain, with its rents, its furrows and
scars, its blackness. The sun is only temporarily effective, and in its
brilliance the mountain's bleakness is exposed. It will be imprisoned
again in the snow. David's assistance to Saul is likely to be only temporary. Saul's grievances will return, as the Biblical story makes so
clear in its emphasis upon "*whenever* the evil spirit from God was
upon Saul."

The final dramatic image suggests permanence and eternality—a
distinct contrast to the temporarily efficacious work of the sun (and
of David). Saul cannot be totally cured on the human or physical
level. He needs a vision of the spiritual, of Love, Power, and
Immortality. He must be able to hope, in the midst of his struggles,

for a fulfilling tomorrow in which he will be greeted by Incarnate Love. David, unable to comprehend anything beyond a human personality, yet feeling a reality beyond, evisions Christ as man's highest conception of love.

Thus, in what appears to be a dramatic poem, Browning reiterates the method and content of his longer religious poem, *Christmas-Eve and Easter-Day*. Beginning with personal needs and desires, moving outward through a sense of one's limitations to examine alternate forms of belief and behavior, he concludes with a vision of Love Incarnate. Saul's misery as an isolated ruler and David's helplessness to assist him underscore Browning's conviction that every man approaches life's ultimate question alone. Faith cannot be shared. But a man cannot tolerate total solitude. His being needs companionship, acceptance, mutual involvement—love. Love shares, encourages, saves. "Love bears all things, believes all things, hopes all things, endures all things. Love never ends."[16] Browning's incantations to love prove his profound awareness of man's loneliness before the universe. David has shared all that one man can give another; his love for Saul is an earnest of Divine Love which sustains the universe and calls Saul into a future of Love.

An examination of the speakers in Browning's religious dramatic monologues demonstrates the singular consistency with which he insists upon their assuming an existential posture. Each speaker— whether he be Caliban, Bishop Blougram, Pope Innocent, Mr. Sludge, or the rest of Browning's cast of characters—always begins subjectively, referring each question to the final judgment of his own being, relinquishing authority to no one else, even God. Two speakers who might seem to be exceptions to this generalization actually strengthen Browning's case. Cleon and Karshish seem remarkably objective in their scientific-rational considerations of religion and of the Christ-event; they reject Christ because the evidence for him is inadequately substantiated. The reader understands, however, that they have impoverished themselves in this rejection, because they have refused the testimony of their inner beings. A clear example of the typical and acceptable existential posture is that of the Pope in *The Ring and the Book*. Pope Innocent believes that the truth cannot be finally embodied in institutions or dogmas; hence he relies upon more personal criteria, his own qualifications as judge. Whether that judgment concerns the guilt or innocence of Guido and Caponsacchi or the existence of God,

16. I Corinthians 13:7, 8. Revised Standard Version.

the method and basis for judgment remain the same. Believing that a portion of the truth may be grasped by human reason from empirical evidence, he nevertheless must trust the impulses of his heart as much as his mind in ascertaining the fullest possible truth.

One dramatic monologue should be singled out for special comment, because of its apparent reliance upon reason and historical evidence to defend Browning's faith. *A Death in the Desert* has been called Browning's "most closely reasoned *apologia* for Christianity, with the possible exception of The Pope in *The Ring and the Book*."[17] David Shaw calls Browning's John a "rationalist, who tries to establish the transcendent logic of a 'love' behind 'the will and might,'" and claims that Browning's intent is to prove that "this logic requires, for reasons of inherent persuasiveness and on grounds of sheer dialectical symmetry alone, the authenticity of the Christian narrative."[18] Browning's John, like most of his religious apologists, does develop his defense in non-Christian language and logical thought patterns, separating the Christian gospel's essence from accoutrements of myth, but his rationalistic argumentation does not build on rationalistic presuppositions. His final arbiter is not reason but personal experience. The Apostle makes no appeal to ecclesiastical dogma or historical evidence (apart from his own account) or supernatural miracle to defend his belief in Christ. His defense is subjective and pragmatic. John's basic argument parallels Browning's words to Mrs. Orr: "But I am none the less convinced that the life and death of Christ, as Christians apprehend them, supply something which their humanity requires, and that it is true for them."[19]

Browning's emphasis upon the personal basis for faith, his reverence for the Christ-event as "something which their humanity requires," and the hint of the relativity of truth to personal experience are all found in John's defense. He must answer two basic charges about his Gospel: (1) The Divine Love about which he writes may be nothing more than the projection of the human heart. From man's earliest times, he has read his own desires and characteristics into the forces of nature; but in his mental maturity, he has discarded these anthropomorphisms for a more intelligent concept of law. Is John's story, as it sounds, an atavistic return to earlier projections? (2) If

17. William Clyde DeVane, *A Browning Handbook*, p. 298.
18. David Shaw, *Dialectical Temper*, p. 185.
19. Quoted in Roma A. King, Jr., *The Focusing Artifice: The Poetry of Robert Browning*, pp. 125–126.

John's tale is true, why is evidence of its truth so weak? Why cannot men know for certain that God has spoken through Christ?

John answers both questions by referring to the nature of man. To John, "man was made to grow, not stop." At each stage of his development, he receives such assistance as he needs—but never more than he needs. At one time, miracles (and not mere human projections) were needed to substantiate the faith; they are no longer necessary—in fact, they would hinder further growth—so they have been withdrawn. Distinguishing between faith and knowledge, John insists that full knowledge thwarts and doubt increases growth. Man was made for struggle, not certainty. God knows; man would but cannot know. The distinction is vital:

> —Man is not God but hath God's end to serve,
> A master to obey, a course to take,
> Somewhat to cast off, somewhat to become?
> Grant this, then man must pass from old to new,
> From vain to real, from mistake to fact,
> From what once seemed good, to what now proves best.
> How could man have progression otherwise?
>
> [542–548]

In humble acceptance of his humanity, then, man can grow. John finds men dynamic, energetic, eager for progress. He bases his argument on his concept of man, arguing from man to God. He does not employ traditional deductive arguments, deducing man's characteristics as the image of God from God himself. John slips easily from the indicative of description into the imperative of prescription: since man progresses, he must progress; since he struggles, he must struggle. It is but a short step then to say that since man is weak, he must be weak for a purpose; since he is subjected to trials, the trials must be necessary; since his knowledge is limited, there must be a reason for his ignorance. That purpose, the apostle asserts, is to assist man to progress. The reasoning is circuitous and logically meaningless. As apology, the poem is a logical failure. However, as testimony of faith based upon personal experience, it is moving and meaningful. While it fails rationally, it nonetheless demonstrates again Browning's unvarying reliance upon subjective religious experience and his implicit conviction that such experience is practically incommunicable and certainly rationally undemonstrable. John is unable to answer his critics' arguments, except by shifting the ground of debate from objective to subjective criteria. Only if his auditors will accept John's presupposition that man is made for progress can they then follow him into his epistemological discussion and validation of the Christ-event. What John really communicates is not the logical consistency of his position, but the existential immediacy of his decision to believe in and to live for Christ. For him the Christ-event is not something that was—"to me, it is; / —Is, here and now: I apprehend nought else."

In addition to his poems, Browning has provided another evidence of his understanding of religious faith. In 1851, he honored the request of Edward Moxon, the publisher of his *Bells and Pomegranates,* to write an introductory essay to *Letters of Percy Bysshe Shelley.* The volume, printed in early 1852, was never distributed, because the letters were discovered to be spurious. The importance of the *Essay,* which Browning never reprinted, was noted by F. J. Furnivall, who had it printed as the first of *The Browning Society's Papers* in 1881. Generally considered the poet's clearest prose statement on the nature of poetry, the *Essay* likewise contains a revealing summary of his concept of the nature of Christianity. Speaking always of Shelley, Browning nevertheless praises him for values which he himself holds.

The *Essay* discusses two kinds of poets, the subjective ("seer") and the objective ("fashioner"), careful not to rank one above the other. While Browning's bias toward the subjective as the "ultimate requirement of every age" is apparent, he insists also upon the value of the objective: "For it is with this world, as starting point and basis alike, that we shall always have to concern ourselves: the world is not to be learned and thrown aside, but reverted to and relearned. The spiritual comprehension may be infinitely subtilised, but the raw material it operates upon, must remain." Nevertheless, he turns "with stronger needs" from a discussion of the objective poet to the subjective one, for he can perceive "the supreme Intelligence which apprehends all things in their absolute truth," being concerned with "not what man sees, but what God sees—the *Ideas* of Plato," not "with the combination of humanity in action, but with the primal elements of humanity." He prefers "to seek them in his own soul as the nearest reflex of that absolute Mind, according to the intuitions of which he desires to perceive and speak." The objective poet concentrates upon the doings of men, "while the subjective poet, whose study has been himself," appeals "through himself to the absolute Divine mind," preferring "to dwell upon those external scenic appearances which strike out most abundantly and uninterruptedly his inner light and power, [he] selects that silence of the earth and sea in which he can best hear the beating of his individual heart, and leaves the noisy, complex, yet imperfect exhibitions of nature in the manifold experience of man around him, which serve only to distract and suppress the working of his brain." Browning appreciates both a realistic and idealistic approach to poetry, either the objective or the subjective "faculty in its eminent state . . . doubtless conceded by Providence as a best gift to men." There is no reason, he argues, why "these two modes of poetic faculty may not issue hereafter from the same poet in successive perfect works." Beyond any doubt, he envisions himself as such an artist, capable of attention to minute physical detail and equally able to withdraw from external appearances to "hear the beating of his individual heart," and through his heart to perceive "the supreme Intelligence which apprehends all things." When Browning turns, almost parenthetically, to consider Shelley's moral and spiritual life, the same objective-subjective polarity colors his thinking, as does his preference for the subjective or intuitive. Noting Shelley's early desire to "see" and to "contrive," he criticizes him for endeavoring "to realise as he went on idealising," because in this departure from the ideal to the real "suddenly he stood pledged to the defence of a set of miserable little expedients, just as if they represented great principles." He has wrongheadedly attacked great principles simply for being antagonistic to his prescribed remedies for wrongs which his "miserable little expedients" were proposed to correct. Thus he mistook "Churchdom for Christianity," and "'the sale of love' and the law of sexual oppression" for marriage. However, according to Browning, he gradually and correctly raised himself "above the contemplation of spots and the attempt at effacing them, to the great Abstract Light," and through "the discrepancy of the creation" he climbed "to the sufficiency of the First Cause."[20]

It is in the context of this praise for Shelley's growth away from the manifold variety of human expedients and physical discrepancies to the one truth that Browning offers his startling appraisal of Shelley's faith—an opinion humorously (and not unjustly) compared to Cardinal Wiseman's opinion that Browning himself might become a Catholic.[21]

20. "Essay on Shelley," *The Four Ages of Poetry, Etc.*, edited by H. F. B. Brett-Smith, pp. 65–79.

21. Ward, *Robert Browning and His World*, p. 196.

I shall say what I think,—had Shelley lived he would have finally ranged himself with the Christians; his very instinct for helping the weaker side (if numbers make strength), his very "hate of hate," which at first mistranslated itself to delirious Queen Mab notes and the like, would have got clearer-sighted by exercise. The preliminary step to following Christ, is the leaving of the dead to bury their dead—not clamouring on His doctrine for an especial solution of difficulties which are referable to the general problem of the universe. Already he had attained to a profession of "a worship to the Spirit of good within, which requires (before it sends that inspiration forth, which impresses its likeness upon all it creates) devoted and disinterested homages, *as Coleridge says*,"—and Paul likewise.

Later he adds:

Meantime, as I call Shelley a moral man, because he was true, simple-hearted, and brave, and because what he acted so corresponded to what he knew, so I call him a man of religious mind, because every audacious negative cast up by him against the Divine, was interpenetrated with a mood of reverence and adoration,—and because I find him everywhere taking for granted some of the capital dogmas of Christianity, while most vehemently denying their historical basement.[22]

Here, in a biographical sketch of another poet, Browning characterizes his own faith. Having expressed his impatience with the "miserable little expedients" of the many forms of religious expression, and of the limitations of all rationalistic or objectified bases of faith in *Christmas-Eve and Easter-Day*, he praises Shelley for his growth toward Browning's position. When one fixes his faith upon reality which transcends earth's circumference, he can then avoid the confusions of the early Shelley. Christianity's essence will not be limited to its physical expressions in the Church; marriage will reveal itself as more than bondage and sexual oppression; the First Cause will assume its rightful pre-eminence over creation's discrepancies; Christianity will be freed from "historical basement." Important in all of this is the mood of the believer: his "instinct for helping the weaker side," his acceptance of life's givens, his worship of the "Spirit of good within," his humility and reverence before the limitless Divine.

22. "Essay on Shelley," 78–79.

This is Browning's familiar emphasis upon personal, individualistic, ahistorical, active, nondoctrinal Christianity. The fellowship of Christians, in order to include Shelley on Browning's terms, cannot be restricted to those who claim church membership, who hold the observance of the sacraments as central to obedience to Christ, or who demand any pledge of allegiance to creed or dogma. Christianity, as Browning defines it, is more an attitude than a church. It is an inward intuition straining through the inequities and evils of earthly existence toward eternal Truth. In the struggle, nothing external can save one—even God. The choice is personal. One is alone; he must decide for himself, then act. He asserts himself upon his universe—not in arrogance, but in humility. Listening to the impulses of his heart, he chooses to believe.

The Experimental Method

If Robert Browning were as purely subjective as the preceding chapter might lead one to believe, the search for his religious faith could be quickly concluded. He could be classified among the Romantic Neoplatonists who rely solely upon intuition and some vague Ideas of Absolute Truth or Goodness to express an intensely personal, empirically unverifiable faith. That there is a strong neoplatonic strain in Browning has already been noted. But the confusion over Browning's religion arises in part from a failure to grasp the paradox in his faith. In fact, the modernity of Browning's faith consists in just this paradox: he holds in uneasy tension both an existential and an experimental (that is, "scientific") attitude. As an existentialist, his faith is subjective, intuitive, based upon pragmatic choice rather than philosophical or religious principle, imposing order upon his world rather than submitting to an order already found there. As an empiricist, he subjects his own and several other religious ideas to analysis, experimentation, comparison, and dialectical confrontation, hoping thereby to prove and justify his position. Constantly aware of the inadequacies of human knowledge and intelligence, perhaps unaware of his inability to move out of his thought patterns, he consciously and sometimes subconsciously projects his personal convictions into concrete events and other personalities in order to test his ideas and intuitions. Browning's faith is no escapist's flight from harsh daily realities. He is unfairly caricatured by critics like Douglas Bush, who writes that "Browning, lustily buffeting the waves of flux, solves all problems by shouting 'God! Life! Love!'"[1] or Esmé Wingfield-

1. *Mythology and the Romantic Tradition in English Poetry*, p. 85.

Stratford, who oversimplifies the faith of Browning as "his robust confidence that you had only to march breast forward for clouds to break and right to triumph."[2] Browning is never this confident. Relying upon his existential faith because he has no other option, he shows in several of his poems that the leap of faith upon which he bases his life is never devoid of doubt. In his poems, the clouds seldom break, and right almost never triumphs on earth. He affirms a life beyond death partially to gain the courage to continue to the struggle now. On earth, evil must be faced—and faced down. One's religion is so important in life's struggle, that he must be as certain as possible that it is viable. The same skepticism that convinces Browning to trust intuition in religious matters similarly demands that he be repeatedly testing his conclusions against all possible alternatives and every possible objection. This existential empiricism corresponds to the paradoxically existential and scientific quality of twentieth-century religious life.

Browning is by no means a pioneer in testing his beliefs in the crucible of experience. His vigorous examination of his concept of Christianity makes him spiritually akin, for instance, to two great Renaissance writers whose concern for the meaning of virtue equalled Browning's for a virtuous faith. Spenser's Belphoebe defines the rigorous way of virtue in terms which foreshadow Browning:

> In woods, in waves, in warres, she wonts to dwell,
> And will be found with perill and with paine;
> Ne can the man, that moulds in idle cell
> Unto her happy mansion attaine:
> Before her gate high God did Sweat ordain.[3]

Milton, in his *Areopagitica,* defends active virtue in terms which parallel Browning's defense of life's struggle for meaning and virtue: "I cannot praise a fugitive and cloistered virtue, unexercised and unbreathed, that never sallies out and seeks her adversary, but shrinks out of the race where that immortal garland is to be run for not without dust and heat."[4] The struggles of which Spenser and Milton write, however, remain within a structured Christian context. They know the meaning of Christian virtue because they are convinced of the

---

2. *Those Earnest Victorians,* pp. 321–322.

3. Quoted in Maurice Evans, *English Poetry in the Sixteenth Century,* second ed., p. 13.

4. *Ibid.*

existence, sovereignty, and revelation of God. For Browning, a transcendental law-giving, prophet-inspiring God is no longer possible.
As a young man, he lost his faith in the traditional doctrines of Christianity, in its institutions, in its rituals and its pietism, in any rationalistic
explanations or enlightened systems, and in the abiding efficacy of
any political activism. In the growing clash between orthodox religion
and its scientific challengers, Browning accepted both the tenets and
the new method of science. Yet he wished to retain as much of his
childhood faith as possible. He could only do so by stripping religion
to its essentials, then submitting those essentials to empirical and pragmatic testing. For him, denominations, schisms, liturgies, buildings,
the literal interpretations of the evangelical pietists or the equally
literal interpretations of the rationalistic demythologizers were secondary considerations. Like Lazarus in *An Epistle . . . of Karshish*, having
once glimpsed eternal truth, he could not be bothered by more mun-
dane considerations.

> He will live, nay, it pleaseth him to live
> So long as God please, and just how God please.
> He even seeketh not to please God more
> (Which meaneth, otherwise) than as God please.
>
> [209–212]

What concerned him most was the pragmatic efficacy of his faith;
it could be most efficacious only if focused on ultimate concerns.
He would have heartily agreed with theologian Paul Tillich that faith
has both a subjective and an objective dimension. According to Tillich,
faith has its personal or mystical quality and its objective, separated
quality:

> Without a preceding experience of the ultimate no faith in the
> ultimate can exist. The mystical type of faith has emphasized
> this point most strongly. Here lies its truth which no theology
> of "mere faith" can destroy. Without the manifestation of God
> in man the question of God and faith in God are not possible.
> There is no faith without participation.
> But faith would cease to be faith without separation—the
> opposite element. He who has faith is separated from the object
> of his faith. Otherwise he would possess it. It would be a mat-
> ter of immediate certainty and not of faith. The "in-spite-of
> element" of faith would be lacking. But the human situation, its

93

finitude and estrangement, prevents man's participation in the ultimate without both the separation and the promise of faith.[5]

As Tillich makes clear, doubt is a "necessary element," a "consequence of the risk of faith." It is necessary, because "serious doubt is confirmation of faith. It indicates the seriousness of the concern, its unconditional character."[6] For Browning, alienated from every traditional religious authority and thrown upon his personal experience of the ultimate, faith includes doubt. Faith defies confirmation—yet demands it. He has chosen his ultimate—God as Love, Love as God—and now he must test it.

To label Browning's dramatic monologue as an experimental or "scientific" method of analyzing religion does not suggest that it is strictly inductive or without a definite point of view. He works with firmly held hypotheses, at times imposing them upon his poems when they do not adequately support his desired conclusions. In the more autobiographical *Christmas-Eve and Easter-Day,* and certainly in the didactic poems of his last years, Browning's *a priori* reasoning distorts his logical development. At his best, however, he can quite successfully detach himself from his subjects and characters. His religious essentials are so few and his curiosity is so great that in his several best monologues he can dramatize sympathetically attitudes which he personally finds inadequate or repugnant. Committed to a Christianity transcending Churchdom, he can analyze the intellectual arguments of various churches and doctrines, portray what it feels like to believe as their adherents believe, and expose their incongruities, cruelties, and absurdities. He achieves this dispassionate distance because, like a sociologist calmly explaining religion with charts and graphs and socio-economic jargon, he does not believe in the religions he is analyzing. He finds truth in them, but the truth is psychological truth adhering to acts of believing, not to formulations or rituals or commentaries. As Robert Langbaum has persuasively demonstrated, the meaning of the dramatic monologue is not in ideas or arguments but in what the speaker comes to perceive. Through the interplay of person, event, context, ideology, and impulse Browning can reflect, corroborate, or justify aspects of his own religious hypotheses while apparently dealing objectively with a character like Caliban or Bishop Blougram.

5. *Dynamics of Faith,* p. 100.
6. *Ibid.,* pp. 18, 22.

Sometimes Browning so successfully maintains objectivity that his readers have been unable to determine from the poems alone what the poet's position is. Early reviews, for example, criticized Browning for defending the morally indefensible Don Juan in *Fifine at the Fair*. One critic praised *Prince Hohenstiel-Schwangau* as a "eulogism on the Second Empire," while another damned it as "a scandalous attack on the old constant friend of England."[7] Readers are still puzzled whether Browning is for or against wily Bishop Blougram, and whether or to what extent *Caliban upon Setebos* is a satire—and against whom. In addition to this objective treatment within individual poems, Browning further tests his ideas and confuses his readers by treating in separate poems characters adhering to several viewpoints. Like Pauline's poet, he is "bound to trust / All feelings equally, to hear all sides." The impartiality he expressed in opening *Dramatic Lyrics* with *Cavalier Tunes*, a denunciation of democratic ideas, and *The Lost Leader*, a denunciation of Toryism and tribute to democracy, compelled him to examine as many sides as possible of major religious issues in his time. He could not content himself with half-truths or one-sided arguments on any subject. Thus, in music, Abt Vogler is an intuitionalist who has caught a glimpse of absolute truth; Charles Avison, on the other hand, takes a relativist's position. In art, Fra Lippo represents exuberant realism and Andrea Del Sarto defends classic idealism. Roman Catholicism is treated tenderly in *The Boy and the Angel*, somewhat cynically in *Bishop Blougram's Apology*, savagely in *Holy-Cross Day*. Ascetic Christianity (*A Death in the Desert*), brutal Calvinism (*Johannes Agricola*), natural theology and Darwinism (*Caliban Upon Setebos*), higher criticism (*Epilogue* to *Dramatis Personae*) are but a few additional religious attitudes he studies. Through this multiplicity of characters and ideas, in which Browning makes it plain where he does not belong, his own position emerges, for one subject does not receive his ironic treatment. To that subject he turns time and again to resolve his intellectual quanderies and moral perplexities. He obviously believes in love. His faith in love's efficacy (in its transcendental and its human and relative dimensions) affords him sufficient psychological and spiritual security to treat other subjects with abandon. Nothing is ultimately sacred that does not help the human personality; nothing helps men and women so much as love. Other claimants for man's religious affections are imposters and should be exposed.

7. Quoted in Robert Langbaum, *The Poetry of Experience*, p. 106.

Browning's repeated testimonies to love and his frequent complaints of the insufficiency of intelligence have misled many readers into dismissing him as anti-intellectual. Critics have accused the poet of harboring an aversion to philosophy or having stunted his intellectual growth or of degrading the intellect because it interferes with his prejudices. All of these accusations imply intellectual cowardice in Browning, a refusal to make his philosophical and religious thinking square with the facts of his experience. Yet it is precisely his reliance upon experience and his intellectual agility that led him to refuse to trust intelligence alone. By thinking, he learned to distrust thinking and to trust his feelings. With his mind he studied systems and theories and doctrines—to find them totally inadequate. These intellectual systems did not sufficiently account for all the facets of man's experience. There are deep yearnings within man which the mind can neither explain nor satisfy.

Browning's rejection of salvation by mind alone did not, however, lead him to an opposite position of anarchical subjectivity. The passions cannot go unchecked by reason. In spite of some hyperbolic statements in his later poetry (such as one from *A Pillar at Sebzevar* in *Ferishtah's Fancies*: "Wholly distrust thy knowledge, then, and trust / As wholly love allied to ignorance!") which, taken out of the context of his whole body of poetry, seem to support a strictly emotional approach to life, Browning's entire corpus blends passion and intelligence to a remarkable degree. To an era enslaved by exaggerated notions of propriety and restraint, Browning enthusiastically proclaimed the goodness of the liberated heart. But he always justified his stand by reference to human experience. Again, his religious reasoning parallels that of Paul Tillich, whose thoughts on the relationship of faith and reason succinctly summarize almost all of Browning's many poems on this subject. Tillich also views man's spiritual life as a unity, with all "spiritual elements" of man within each other:

> Reason is the precondition of faith; faith is the act in which
> reason reaches ecstatically beyond itself. This is the opposite
> side of their being within each other. Man's reason is finite; it
> moves within finite relations when dealing with the universe and
> with man himself . . . But reason is not bound to its own finitude.
> It is aware of it and, in so doing, rises above it. Man experiences
> a belonging to the infinite which, however, is neither a part
> of himself nor something in his power. It must grasp him, and if
> it does, it is a matter of infinite concern. Man is finite, man's

96

reason lives in preliminary concerns; but man is also aware of his potential infinity, and this awareness appears as his ultimate concern, his faith. If reason is grasped by an ultimate concern, it is driven beyond itself; but it does not cease to be reason, finite reason. The ecstatic experience of an ultimate concern does not destroy the structure of reason. Ecstasy is fulfilled, not denied, rationality. Reason can be fulfilled only if it is driven beyond the limits of its finitude, and experiences the presence of the ultimate, the holy.[8]

Like Tillich, Browning does not attack intelligence *per se,* but intelligence as the sole measure of truth. The mind must join the heart and conscience in spiritual experience, not repress or delimit them. It must appraise, adjust, and articulate the impulses of the heart, but neither deny nor disregard them. Man contains both head and heart, and can live only when both properly interact. All heart leads to spiritual anarchy; all head, to rational tyranny over man's deepest being.

Many examples could be cited to illustrate Browning's understanding of the relation of intelligence and emotion in spiritual considerations, but perhaps the clearest is *Caliban upon Setebos; or, Natural Theology in the Island.* Twenty years after he had written this poem, Browning named it his most representative "dramatic" poem, but the subject and the manner of arguing are so familiar to Browning readers, that George Bernard Shaw spoke for many of them when he complained—accurately, but, at the time, heretically—at a meeting of the Browning Society that "Shakespeare, being a dramatic poet, has never labelled any work of his dramatic; Browning, being essentially undramatic, has called this Caliban poem a dramatic monologue." He faulted Caliban as "unnatural, impossible, and radically undramatic."[9] Shaw's abrupt dismissal of all Browning's work as essentially undramatic depends upon the meaning of the term, of course, but in one respect it is a correct judgment on *Caliban.* It appears in the 1864 *Dramatis Personae,* in which Browning's dramatic mask is more transparent than in the 1855 *Men and Women,* and he deals more directly and polemically with current theological controversies. *Mr. Sludge, "the Medium,"* for instance, is Browning's statement on

8. *Dynamics of Faith,* pp. 76–77.

9. Quotes in Maisie Ward, *Robert Browning and His World: Two Robert Brownings?,* p. 16.

the spiritualist craze infecting England and the Continent (and which Browning observed at close range because of his wife's intense interest in it); *A Death in the Desert* deals at least in part with the attacks of higher criticism on the authorship of the fourth gospel. *Caliban* takes its place among them, differing from them and earlier poems in the unusually complex interweaving of several theological concerns, including natural theology, Darwinism, Calvinism, anthropomorphism, and institutional faith.

Caliban ostensibly satirizes natural theology, with its rationalistic attempts to account for God as simply anthropomorphic projections. "Thou thoughtest that I was altogether such a one as thyself," reads the motto from Psalms 50:21. Caliban, a despicable subhuman creature whose strongest emotions are fear, envy, hatred, and vindictiveness, cannot conceive of his god Setebos in any other terms. Being so aware of the evil within himself and his observable world, he concludes that the author of this evil must be miserable himself, avenging his misery by making his creatures equally unhappy: "He made all these and more, / Made all we see, and us, in spite: how else?" This he can do, for "He is strong and Lord," arbitrarily and capriciously flexing his muscles: "Let twenty pass, and stone the twenty-first, / Loving not, hating not, just choosing so." In one act he is not capricious. Having made some creatures "worthier than Himself," he envies them—and demands complete obedience from them, else, "Would not I smash it with my foot? So He."

To account for his misery by projecting an equally miserable god places Caliban in a dilemma, however. His God cannot be all-powerful, or he could change himself and eliminate the evil which torments him. So Caliban must further postulate a god above his god:

> But wherefore rough, why cold and ill at ease?
> Aha, that is the question! Ask, for that,
> What knows,—the something over Setebos
> That made Him, or He, may be found and fought,
> Worsted, drove off and did to nothing, perchance.
> There may be something quiet o'er His head,
> Out of His reach, that feels nor joy nor grief,
> Since both derive from weakness in some way.
> I joy because the quails come; would not joy
> Could I bring quails here when I have a mind:
> This Quiet, all it hath a mind to, doth.

[127–137]

With this speculation, Caliban is intellectually satisfied. He can account for Setebos's spiteful, unpredictable behavior. He can likewise satisfy his own moral demands that there be some good principle in the universe to correspond to his outraged sense of worth (knowing that Setebos "hath made things worthier than Himself.") That principle he names Quiet. Thus, from empirical evidence, Caliban proves the power of Setebos; from his own motives and behavior, he projects Setebos's characteristics; from his intellectual reasonings, he deduces the concept of Quiet. It is a neat system. Its only fault is that it does not work, at least for Caliban. Quiet may be infinite, but it is also impersonal. It is very well for Caliban, groping for some rational explanation for his universe, to posit a Quiet to account for a Setebos, but such a theory in no way changes things nor assists Caliban. He needs relief from anxiety, a relationship of love, and not impersonal unconcern or an abstract principle. The Quiet can explain Setebos but cannot help Caliban. The only god Caliban knows is Setebos. His reasoning leads him to a familiar dead end: "If Setebos is God, then God is not good; if the Quiet is God, then God is not God. Since either Setebos or the Quiet is divine, God cannot be good and omnipotent at the same time."[10]

For Browning, the test of belief is behavior, not words. Caliban's real worship, then, is not in his carefully reasoned analysis, but in his frightened prostration when the argument is over. Self-incrimination, desperate fear, careless sacrifice mark his religious observance. Deeper than all the rationalization lies an instinctive awe before raw natural force, a wonder which no amount of ratiocination can efface. The Darwinians may be quite right in postulating an evolutionary process by which man developed from simpler, Caliban-like beasts, but Browning intimates that we have not left behind Caliban's primitive, intuitive, essential need to worship. The rationalists may correctly complain at the abundance of anthropomorphisms in religious vocabulary, but all men, like Caliban, must use the only conceptual tools at their disposal to refer to their sense of the divine. The Calvinists and the natural theologians perpetrate the identical sin in speaking so confidently about their systematized knowledge of God. They are, like Caliban, limited to physical evidences and human vocabulary and thought patterns. Although they also, like Caliban, must account for their faith as far as their intelligence will

---

10. David Shaw, *The Dialectical Temper: The Rhetorical Art of Robert Browning*, p. 201.

allow, Browning insists that they must become aware of the limitations of that intelligence. In Caliban, then, reasoning is revealed as rationalization—a necessary, but limited human expedient. Faith is not something we say; it is not a series of propositions to which we assent. It is what we do.

The relation of intelligence to faith is made quite clear also in the *Epilogue* to *Dramatis Personae*. As in *Christmas-Eve and Easter-Day*, Browning presents alternatives, rejects them, then submits his own solution. The structure of the *Epilogue* is dialectical, with the first two speakers representing religious attitudes quite opposed to each other. David speaks for the ritualistic, sacerdotal attitude which finds God housed in a sanctuary—the House of the Lord, either Church or Synagogue. The second speaker, Renan, represents Browning's judgment on the higher critics in particular (especially Strauss and Renan, the latter of whom he had probably just read[11]) and the entire skeptical, rationalistic attitude growing in the nineteenth century. Browning's Renan grieves that his great historical knowledge has driven any faith in the historical Christ from him. The "face" which once looked down upon men, the star which has receded into the multitude of lesser lights, is gone. Browning rejects the ritualistic position as impractical and unnecessary—and as intellectually indefensible. He rejects the rationalistic contention that greater historical knowledge will cause Christ to vanish; for him, "That one Face, far from vanish, rather grows." Through the increase of knowledge, it "decomposes but to recompose, / Because my universe that feels and knows." In the poem's last line, a copula unites "Feels" and "knows," summarizing Browning's union of thought and emotion in religious experience.

When Browning speaks for himself in the third section, he does so to correct the others who are "Witless alike of will and way divine." They have not perceived "How heaven's high with earth's low should intertwine!" Although Browning has elsewhere emphasized the vast

11. See his letter (of November 19, 1863) to Miss Isa Blagden in *Dearest Isa: Robert Browning's Letters to Isabella Blagden,* edited by Edward C. McAleer, p. 180. "I have just read Renan's book, and find it weaker and less honest than I was led to expect. I am glad it is written: if he thinks he can prove what he says, he has fewer doubts on the subject than I—but mine are none of his . . . The want of candour is remarkable: you could no more deduce the character of his text from the substance of his notes, than rewrite a novel from simply reading the mottoes at the head of each chapter . . . Take away every claim to man's respect from Christ and then give him a wreath of gum-roses and calico-lilies."

gulf between the Divine and the human, he here stresses another aspect of his faith: the relationship between the divine and the human. The ritualist and the rationalist are both wrong in minimizing the individuality and the worth of each human being. The individual's participation in nature's force is illustrated by reference to the Arctic Seas, which seem instinctively to flee toward a rock, encircle it with radiance and playfulness, uproot it, and then "hasten off to play again elsewhere." This, says Browning, is how nature dances:

> About each man of us, retire, advance,
> As though the pageant's end were to enhance
>
> IX
>
> His worth, and—once the life, his product, gained—
> Roll away elsewhere, keep the strife sustained,
> And show thus real, a thing the North but feigned—
>
> X
>
> When you acknowledge that one world could do
> All the diverse work, old yet evernew,
> Divide us, each from other, me from you,—
>
> XI
>
> Why, where's the need of Temple, when the walls
> O' the world are that? What use of swells and falls
> From Levites' choir, Priests' cries, and trumpet-calls?
>
> XII
>
> That one Face, far from vanish, rather grows,
> Or decomposes but to recompose,
> Become my universe that feels and knows.
>
> [88–101]

God is everywhere in the universe, immediately accessible to every worshipper without priestly intercession. Christ, rather than vanishing through historical research, becomes more vivid to the individual worshipper through immediate experience. Browning has not really answered the higher critics on their own grounds. He has shifted from examination of historical data to the testimony of the worthy individual's feelings, data much more relevant to religious expression than any scientific facts could be. The "Face" he sees, he once explained to Mrs. Orr, "is the face of Christ. That is how I feel him."[12] He has moved from a somewhat objective statement of opposing religious attitudes, intelligently and dispassionately set forth, through a metaphysical simile expressing his own premise of man's worth, to a confession of his faith based upon that premise. Browning's apprehension of his universe must be "reasonable." It must account as far as possible for all phenomena, natural and psychological. Then and only then can it leap beyond man's finitude to assert itself upon the infinite. This is the method of the *Epilogue*.

In *An Epistle . . . of Karshish* Browning presents one who, like Renan and Caliban, has carefully examined scientific and logical evidence, but who cannot make the necessary leap of faith. Karshish is one of Browning's most appealing characters—and, one suspects, one who most resembles Browning in his preliminary approach to religious questions. Although the poem is ostensibly about the interview of the Arab physician with Lazarus, whom Christ raised from the dead, the poem's center of interest is in Karshish. He possesses Browning's characteristics as one "not-incurious in God's handiwork"—one sensitive to religious experience, and as "the picker-up of learning's crumbs" —a factual scientist, a logical thinker. These two characteristics, as we have noted, do not abide easily with each other. As a religious scientist, Karshish approaches all new knowledge humbly and curiously, eager to learn. He confesses, amid his apologies for his prolixity and for the improbability of his story about Lazarus, that "awe indeed this man has touched me with." Lazarus has experienced what Karshish yearns for, yet cannot quite accept. For him Lazarus remains a madman. Karshish's final words bespeak his reaching out toward God, his deep theistic faith, and his need for a personal relationship with a personal God. But he cannot accept God on the evidence of a madman; nor can he accept his testimony just because his heart wants to. So he concludes with words which echo David's ecstasy in *Saul* in everything but assent:

> The very God! think, Abib; dost thou think?
> So, the All-great, were the All-Loving too—
> So, through the thunder comes a human voice
> Saying, "O heart I made, a heart beats here!
> Face, my hands fashioned, see it in myself!

12. Mrs. Sutherland Orr, "The Religious Opinions of Robert Browning," *Contemporary Review*, p. 880. In DeVane, *Handbook*, p. 315.

Thou hast no power nor mayst conceive of mine,
But love I gave thee, with myself to love,
And thou must love me who have died for thee!"
The madman saith He said so: it is strange.

[304–312]

Karshish differs from Browning, and in this difference is found Browning's resolution to Karshish's intellectual difficulty. Karshish readily concedes the appeal of Lazarus's story of a God of love who sacrificed himself for man. Karshish, as a healer and believer, wants to believe in a God who, in a stroke of love, becomes human and heals with his divine blood. To do so, however, he must accept the testimony of an obviously abnormal personality. The tale is so strange that Karshish doubts its historicity. His doubt paralyzes him; he cannot act on what he has heard. His letter ends in a suspension of belief.

The conclusions of *Karshish* and the *Epilogue* make very clear Browning's approach to the data of faith. No more able than Karshish to resolve doubts about the historicity of Lazarus's tale, he would nonetheless have appropriated it in faith, because it answers the deepest needs of the heart. Karshish is correct in submitting the story to intellectual analysis; he fails only in not also trusting the desires of his heart, in not accepting the testimony of his intuitions as well as that of his senses.

Karshish's description of himself as both scientist and religious seeker surprisingly resembles that of a prominent twentieth-century evolutionist and theologian, Pierre Teilhard de Chardin, whose writings offer a helpful commentary upon Browning's application of the experimental method to questions of faith. In his recently published *How I Believe*, he describes himself almost as Karshish does:

> The originality of my belief lies in its being rooted in two domains of life which are commonly regarded as antagonistic. By upbringing and intellectual training, I belong to the "children of heaven"; but by temperament, and by my professional studies, I am a "child of the earth." Situated thus by life at the heart of two worlds with whose theory, idiom, and feelings intimate experience has made me familiar, I have not erected any watertight bulkhead inside myself. On the contrary, I have allowed two apparently conflicting influences full freedom to react upon one another deep within me. And now, at the end of that operation, after thirty years devoted to the pursuit of interior unity, I

103

have the feeling that a synthesis has been effected naturally between the two currents that claim my allegiance. The one has
not destroyed, but has reinforced, the other. Today I believe
probably more profoundly than ever in God, and certainly more
than ever in the world.[13]

Teilhard's little book develops the logical steps through which he
has arrived at his twofold belief. His words sound more like Browning
than Karshish. Karshish is unable to step toward belief in Christ
because of the insufficiency of the testimony and the testifier; Teilhard,
who spent his lifetime examining earth's testimony, begins precisely
where Browning does, with the individual, although he goes beyond
Browning in arriving finally at the position of the Roman Catholic
Church. Trusting fully the evidence of his own being and presupposing that "man is essentially the same in all of us, and we have only
to look sufficiently deeply within ourselves to find a common sub-
stratum of aspirations and illumination," he states his thesis: "It is
through that which is most incommunicably personal in us that we
make contact with the universal." His reliance upon the personal,
says this believing scientist, is inescapable: "The essential note of the
psychological act of faith is to perceive as possible, and accept as
more probable, a conclusion which, in spatial width or temporal exten-
tion, cannot be contained in any analytical premises. *To believe is to
effect an intellectual synthesis*." To achieve this synthesis, he descends
step by step to his fundamental intuition "below which I can no longer
distinguish anything at all." He then reverses the process and re-
ascends "the natural series . . . of my successive acts of faith in the
direction of an over-all view which ultimately is found to coincide
with Christianity." He explains the importance of this process in words
which describe Browning's method: "First one has to verify the solidity
of an inevitable initial fatih, and then one has to verify the organic
continuity of the successive stages which the augmentations of that
faith pass through."[14] As the third and fourth chapters of this paper
attempt to demonstrate, Browning's procedure is the same as
Teilhard's. Having found an "I" in whom he can believe, Browning
then verifies his growth through objective and intellectual tests.
Karshish cannot join them. Although he is painfully aware of his

13. Translated by Rene Hague, pp. 10–11. Originally written in Peking, 1934, but
unpublished until 1969.
14. *Ibid.*, pp. 12–16.

inner yearnings, an important part of his "I," he does not fully trust them. He builds upon fragmentary empirical reality, "learning's crumbs," rather than upon an intellectual synthesis with his soul as its basis. For him, then, the Christ-event can never be more than one more bit of information, one more interesting phenomenon examined and catalogued—strange, suggestive, but not persuasive. For Browning, no more able to verify its historicity than is Karshish, it possesses psychological and spiritual truth because it corresponds to the intuitions of his inner being and it passes the comparative and analytical tests to which his experience submits it. Its historicity, an interesting but academic question, is secondary to its powerful ability to respond to the heart's demands. Karshish places his faith in his senses and his mind; Browning places it in his soul, which includes and transcends his senses, mind, and heart.

When all Browning's religious poems are compared, not only do his fusion of intellect and faith and his subordination of intellect to the soul emerge, but also his motive for returning so frequently to this theme. Writing in the tradition of John Milton, but in answer to the new demands of a secularized intellectual milieu, he does not "justify the ways of God to man" so much as he justifies the ways of Browning to men. Reasoning readily becomes rationalization. What appears to be a thorough survey of the fallacies and fallibilities of orthodox religion (as in *Christmas-Eve and Easter-Day* and *Epilogue* to *Dramatis Personae*), or an examination of the limitations of human thought and endeavor (*Karshish, Cleon, Saul, Caliban*) is in fact a lifetime brief prepared to defend his own position. To be a theist in the nineteenth century was to stick stubbornly to an increasingly challenged attitude. One who, like Browning, determined to believe found himself increasingly on the defensive. Empiricists demanded proof of God which could satisfy empirical standards. Such proof could not be given. In his poems, Browning does not ever accept the challenge to prove empirically that God is. To the contrary, his poems testify that God cannot be fully apprehended by man. So Browning has fastened upon what can be known: the feelings of the inner self, the needs and desires for faith, hope, and love. He has placed his faith in love and has chosen to hope for a greater experience of that love in the future. He has personified it in his personal concept of Christ. Then he has taken his stand. The search is over. The monologues do not offer any new information or clues about God. Rather, they demonstrate the existential nature of man's faith, his ability to manipulate God-language for his own exigencies, and his ultimate reliance upon his own authority. The speakers in the poems—like Karshish—never change their minds; there are no conversions to Christ among them. They betray a passion to redeem themselves in the eyes of their peers. They are, in fact, like Browning. They all protest that they are living by definite inner standards, and that they *do* attempt to conform to the highest dictates of their consciences. They are solitary men, justifying their life-styles. And their often subtle, sometimes tortuous, arguments are distortions or approximations or even burlesques of Browning's favorite doctrines.

In all the casuistical reasonings of Browning's monologuists, there is one invariable. They justify themselves by calling God as their witness. They speak with complete assurance of their relation to God. According to G. K. Chesterton, they self-confidently rely upon "the indulgence of divine perfection."

> Thus Sludge is certain that his life of lies and conjuring tricks has been conducted in a deep and subtle obedience to the message really conveyed by the conditions created by God. Thus Bishop Blougram is certain that his life of panic-stricken and tottering compromise has been really justified as the only method that could unite him with God. Thus Prince Hohenstiel-Schwangau is certain that every dodge in his thin string of political dodges has been the true means of realising what he believes to be the will of God. Every one of these meagre swindlers, while admitting a failure in all things relative, claims an awful alliance with the Absolute.[15]

Chesterton defends these "swindlers" by some fancy casuistry, himself. Noting that many would call this confident alliance with God "a dangerous doctrine indeed," he insists that it is really "a most solid and noble and salutary" one, "far less dangerous than its opposite."

> Every one of this earth should believe, amid whatever madness or moral failure, that his life and temperament have some object on the earth. Every one on the earth should believe that he has something to give to the world which cannot otherwise be given. Everyone should, for the good of men and the saving of his own soul, believe that it is possible, even if we are the enemies of the human race, to be the friends of God. The evil

15. *Robert Browning*, pp. 201–202.

wrought by this mystical pride, great as it often is, is like a straw
to the evil wrought by a materialistic self-abandonment.[16]

Chesterton's defense of these casuists is delightfully beside the point.
He ignores any question of the veracity of their claims about God
and makes no reference to absolute ethical standards. His argument
sounds much like Browning's. Based upon man's need for purpose,
on his individuality, and on his sense of relation with a transcendent
being, man's appropriation of God to justify his own existence seems
quite legitimate to Chesterton. Whether even Chesterton could use
this general argument to excuse some specific speakers, such as
Johannes Agricola in *Johannes Agricola in Meditation,* is doubtful. The
exclusively self-centered references to God in this poem and all the
other monologues make Chesterton's assessment of Browning's doctrine as "most solid and noble and salutary" questionable. But these
allusions to God do underscore the human necessity to justify one's
behavior in cosmic terms.

Whereas Johannes and the monk in *Soliloquy in a Spanish Cloister*
draw upon the God-language of Calvinistic or Catholic doctrine to
justify their almost pathological selfishness, Bishop Blougram strips
his language of transcendental overtones, assuming the premises of
his antagonist, Gigadibs. He grants the equally problematic nature
of belief and unbelief, then justifies his choice of belief strictly in
pragmatic, this-worldly terms. He scrupulously avoids any use of doctrine or ecclesiastical tradition. He admits the presence of doubt within
his belief. He even confesses that his ecclesiastical office fulfills his
drive for dominance and his love of comfort:

> There's power in me and will to dominate
> Which I must exercise, they hurt me else:
> In many ways I need mankind's respect,
> Obedience, and the love that's born of fear:
> While at the same time, there's a taste I have,
> A toy of soul, a titillating thing
> Refuses to digest these dainties crude.
>
> [322–328]

The only genuine defense he can offer for his belief in God is his
instinctive need for God:

---

16. *Ibid.,* p. 202.

You own your instincts? why, what else do I,
Who want, am made for, and must have a God
Ere I can be aught, do aught?—no mere name
Want, but the true thing with what proves its truth,
To wit, a relation from that thing to me,
Touching from head to foot—which touch I feel,
And with it take the rest, this life of ours!

[845–851]

It is an agrument more appropriate to William James than to St. Thomas. Finding it impossible to certify his faith objectively, he defines faith more as an act of will than of reason, and validates it pragmatically rather than logically: It is good because of its effect on the believer. In so doing, not only does he answer Gigadibs, but he demonstrates the possibility of religious faith of some sort even in mid-nineteenth-century England, and that in a confrontation of religious faith of any sort with non-faith, the beliver is as powerful as—if not even more powerful than—the nonbeliever. Nonetheless, the Bishop does not convince the reader that his skillful ratiocination is much more than a supremely clever rationalization of a selfish worldly existence. His comfortable life-style is the most satisfying one possible for an erudite, somewhat cynical bishop. His morally ambiguous position is matched by the intellectual ambiguity of his dialectic. He can readily employ half-truths "for argumentatory purposes":

Some arbitrary accidental thoughts
That crossed his mind, amusing because new
He chose to represent as fixtures there.

[984–986]

He does say "true things, but called them by wrong names." In all his words his motivation remains constant:

"On the whole," he thought, "I justify myself
On every point where cavillers like this
Oppugn my life: he tries one kind of fence
I close, he's worsted, that's enough for him."

[997–1000]

The bishop has closed his case.
   This self-justifying motive unites all of Browning's disparate characters. As different as they are from each other in temperament,

108

morality, historical periods, and life-styles, they share a compulsion to explain themselves. And, as Chesterton has observed, they unhesitatingly call God to their defense. They are not all as explicit as Mr. Sludge, who admits that "Sludge is of all-importance to himself." Although all of the characters think as highly of themselves, they cannot all confess their self-regard so openly. Nor can they defend their motives with Sludge's self-assurance:

> I cheat in self-defence,
> And there's my answer to a world of cheats!
>
> [1346–1347]

To make his way in a dishonest world, Sludge embraces the tactics of dishonesty, manipulating appearances and distorting scriptures. Fra Lippo Lippi, on the other hand, as admirable and sympathetic a personality as Mr. Sludge is despicable and conniving, indulges himself in the same kind of self-defense. He justifies his portrayal of real men and women as confidently as Sludge defends his sleights-of-hand:

> If you get simple beauty and nought else,
> You get about the best thing God invents.
>
> [217–218]

> However, you're my man, you've seen the world
> —The beauty and the wonder and the power,
> The shapes of things, their colours, lights and shades,
> Changes, surprises,—and God made it all!
>
> [282–285]

For this conviction that all in the world is God-made, Fra Lippo derives his sense of worth. As an artist he is God's partner. In that partnership he finds meaning and enthusiasm for life:

> For, don't you mark? we're made so that we love
> First when we see them painted, things we have passed
> Perhaps a hundred times nor cared to see;
> And so they are better, painted—better to us,
> Which is the same thing. Art was given for that;
> God uses us to help each other so,
> Lending our minds out.
>
> [300–306]

109

Andrea del Sarto is as bland and defeated as Fra Lippo is ebullient and positive, but he can also speak confidently of God—although in a strangely stoical, half-apologetic tone. Andrea can escape censure for his limited success as an artist by hiding behind a predestinarian God whose will overrides all human struggles against it:

> Love, we are in God's hand.
> How strange, now, looks the life he makes us lead;
> So free we seem, so fettered fast we are!
> I feel he laid the fetter: let it lie!
>
> [48–51]

> All is as God over-rules.
>
> [133]

> At the end,
> God, I conclude, compensates, punishes.
>
> [140–141]

Another believer in God's immediate determination of life's direction is the robust and exceedingly optimistic Rabbi ben Ezra, who welcomes "Each rebuff / That turns earth's smoothness rough." After his tribute to God and the soul ("but thy soul and God stand sure"), the only certainties in life, he concludes with his prayer: "My times be in thy hand! / Perfect the cup as planned!" *Rabbi ben Ezra* is one of Browning's most famous poems and, some believe, one of the clearest statements of Browning's own faith. David Shaw, however, is so skeptical of the genuineness of the Rabbi's God that he calls his "affirmation that he can accomplish all things through God . . . simply the pretense of an ethical man who can do everything by himself and who mimics religious experience by pretending that God helps him."[17] Shaw's reading of *Rabbi ben Ezra* is similar to the suggestion of this chapter. The point is that in all these monologues, the word *God* may refer to a transcendent being, but it more probably serves the self-justifying ends of the speakers. The Rabbi may actually be no more honest in claiming God's help than Sludge is in his boast that he served religion: "With my phenomena / I laid the atheist sprawling on his back." The Bishop, Sludge, the Rabbi, Andrea del

---

17. *The Dialectical Temper*, p. 218.

Sarto, and their fellow monologuists recall Paracelsus, who, in the height of his confidence, claimed without hesitation that he was doing God's will. They recognized one of the strongest virtues of God-language: its accessibility; it can be appropriated at any time to defend almost any human activity. It is the perfect camouflage, hiding the most exaggerated expressions of egoism beneath the foliage of verbal piety. Every conceivable character borrows it. Consequently, through an accumulation of character studies, Browning demonstrates irrefutably the unreliability of God-language, and underscores one of his central convictions: faith has to be what one does, not what one says. "By their fruits ye shall know them," and not by their many self-justifying words.

This discussion of Browning's experimental method takes for granted his remarkable devotion to the things of this world, which marks him as unique among religious poets up to his time. Spenser tests Christian virtue in a fairy land, and Milton justifies the ways of God to man in an elaborate imaginative cosmos. Only Browning, prior to our century, so consistently justifies his other-worldly aspirations with such minute attention to this world's phenomena. "Fairy-poetry," he agreed with Elizabeth Barrett, was "impossible in the days of steam."[18] G. K. Chesterton, with his usual perceptivity, finds Browning's "sense of the symbolism of material trifles" his "supreme peculiarity":

> Enormous problems, and yet more enormous answers, about pain, prayer, destiny, liberty, and conscience are suggested by cherries, by the sun, by a melon-seller, by an eagle flying in the sky, by a man tilling a plot of ground. It is this spirit of grotesque allegory which really characterizes Browning among all other poets. Other poets might possibly have hit upon the same philosophical idea—some ideas as deep, as delicate, and as spiritual. But it may be safely asserted that no other poet, having thought of a deep, delicate, and spiritual idea, would call it "A Bean Stripe; also Apple Eating."[19]

Chesterton could have added that no other poet would have had the audacity—some would say the irreverence—to publish, as an old man, his *Summum Bonum*:

18. Quoted by C. H. Herford, *Robert Browning*, p. 239.
19. *Robert Browning*, pp. 127–128.

All the breath and the bloom of the year in the bag
                    of one bee:
All the wonder and wealth of the mine in the heart
                    of one gem:
In the core of one pearl all the shade and the shine of
                    the sea:
Breath and bloom, shade and shine,—wonder, wealth,
                    and—how far above them—
          Truth, that's brighter than gem,
          Trust, that's purer than pearl,—
Brightest truth, purest trust in the universe—all
                    were for me
In the kiss of one girl.[20]

Whether *Summum Bonum* is simply hyperbole or impersonal lyric or a delightful joke, it is not far from Browning's life-long rhapsody to earth's joys and love's touches. Although he occasionally speaks of love as a Platonic Idea, he really pays only lip-service to it as an abstract absolute. He lives and loves in the concrete present. Undoubtedly, Fra Lippo speaks for Browning when he proclaims

          This world's no blot for us,
     Nor blank; it means intensely, and means good:
     To find its meaning is my meat and drink.

                                        [313–315]

Browning, like Fra Lippo, finds that meaning in flesh and blood, in flowers and busts and bank-accounts. Without sharing Alexander Pope's world-view of essentially deistic theology, he could still agree with Pope's charge to men:

     Know then thyself, presume not God to scan;
     The proper study of Mankind is Man.

Into that study Browning throws himself with enthusiasm, eschewing ethereal speculation about the other world for detailed observation of this world. His characters measure their success by this world's standards. Bishop Blougram, for example, admits his regard for "the creature-comforts" in spite of his ecclesiastical office:

20. From *Asolando: Fancies and Facts.*

I act for, talk for, live for this world now,
As this world prizes action, life and talk:
No prejudice to what next world may prove,
Whose new laws and requirements, my best pledge
To observe then, is that I observe these now,
Shall do hereafter what I do meanwhile.

[769–774]

His Italian Renaissance ancestor in *The Bishop Orders His Tombs at Saint Praxed's Church* has so successfully accumulated this world's goods—jewels and stones—and sons—that even on his deathbed the imminence of the next world scarcely diverts his attention from his earthly resting place.

In spite of his unflagging interest in the treasures of earth, however, Browning does not let his readers forget the basic conclusion of *Easter-Day*. Nature, art, and intellectual attainments are meaningless if this world is all we have. Browning is a connoisseur of life's choicest fruits in foods and books and the arts, but he does not accept the hedonist's belief that men should "eat, drink, and be merry, for tomorrow they die." The offerings of earth give pleasure, he believes, when they are received as temporal symbols of eternal plenitude, God's promise of even greater gifts to come. If life ends at the grave, if beauty and truth and love die with the body, and if the soul is only an earth-bound phenomenon, then should men despair, indeed. Browning illustrates this despair in the letter of his brilliant philosopher and poet, Cleon. Cleon is everything the speaker in *Easter-Day* had hoped to be; he has excelled in sculpture, painting, music, and metaphysics. As Cleon himself says, "In brief, all arts are mine." But he is desperately unhappy. His many accomplishments have been for nought. Trapped by time and body, he feels life ebbing out of him even while his capacity for life grows:

Say rather that my fate is deadlier still,
In this, that every day my sense of joy
Grows more acute, my soul (intensified
By power and insight) more enlarged, more keen;
While every day my hairs fall more and more,
My hand shakes, and the heavy years increase—
The horror quickening still from year to year,
The consummation coming past escape
When I shall know most, and yet least enjoy . . .

113

I, I the feeling, thinking, acting man,
The man who loved his life so over-much
Sleep in my urn. It is so horrible.

[309–317; 321–323]

His soul struggles with his contradictory passions, with his sensitivity
to the physical beauty of nature and man's handiwork challenged
by his equally sensitive awareness of beauty's transitory fragility. In
his agony he dares to hope for a future existence, "unlimited in capability for joy," but he dismisses his dream as folly. He has heard of
a preacher named Paulus whose message includes a promise of a
future existence—but the haughty Greek cannot believe him:

Thou canst not think a mere barbarian Jew
As Paulus proves to be, one circumcized,
Hath access to a secret shut from us?
Thou wrongest our philosophy, O king,
In stooping to inquire of such an one
As if his answer could impose at all!

[343–348]

Cleon, like Karshish, misses his opportunity to learn of the future
life for which he yearns. His sin is not in his worldly pursuits. He
sins in refusing to accept anything but the external evidence of this
world. Again like Karshish, he refuses to trust the yearnings of his
heart. Karshish desires to believe in a God of Love, but refuses to
accept the testimony of Lazarus concerning such a God, because he
doubts Lazarus's sanity.

Cleon yearns for a future as "unlimited in capability for joy" as
this life is unlimited in its "desire for joy," but he rejects the impulses
of his heart, because the doctrine taught by Christ's followers "could
be held by no sane man." In the confrontation between the claims
of Christ and the philosophy of Greek humanism which the poem
presents, Greek humanism is to be faulted for not being human
enough. Cleon is a rationalist, not a humanist in the fullest meaning
of this term. His world is orderly, but it is basically hostile to the
restless, dynamic, creative nature of man. In Cleon's static,
materialistic, and mechanical universe, man is destined to be frus-
trated. He is an exception to the order; he must yield to the eternal
system.

Cleon closely resembles the mechanistic scientist of Browning's time,
who could account for natural phenomena, so long as he did not

114

include man among the phenomena. Implicit in *Cleon* is Browning's long-standing scorn of any systematic philosophy which refuses to center itself in man's nature. Browning's cure for Cleon's despondency is not a prescription that Cleon should leave his occupation with this world's arts; it is rather that he should become even more conscientious in his study of earthly life. He must add the evidence of human life to that of natural life. He will find that human existence implies a transcendental existence which in turn infuses this life with meaning. He will then be able to find solace in the teachings of Paulus, who would teach Cleon a new definition of sanity.

Since Browning bases all his discussions of religious problems in terms of this world, why do not all of his speakers, who have access to the same physical evidence, come to an acceptance of Christianity? It is obvious from Cleon's words, for example, that he could have accepted neither a Christian nor a Greek god. Could any evidence have convinced the skeptical Karshish? Cleon and Karshish are no more intellectual or skeptical than Bishop Blougram, no more rationalistic than Caliban, and certainly more admirable than Mr. Sludge. They are no less sensitive to beauty and to creation's marvels than Fra Lippo and Andrea del Sarto. Why are they unable to believe? Their intuitions are the same as those of all the other speakers. Their inability to believe lies, undoubtedly, in their refusal to acknowledge the contingency of all faith, even theirs. Karshish calls Lazarus a madman and Cleon claims that no sane man could believe in Christian doctrine for the same reason: both men, trusting solely to empirical evidence and rational logic, have arbitrarily excluded the testimonies of their hearts and of the experiences of others. Ensnared by their culture's faith in metaphysical and empirical systems they have concluded their experiments before all the data are in, ignoring those which cannot be scientifically tested. Browning, on the other hand, accepts the necessarily contingent character of faith. Unable to prove God, he lives as if God exists, while still looking for further evidence of His existence. Unable to find indisputable historical evidence of Christ's life and ministry, he accepts them as if they were true. Unable to prove that there is life beyond death, he hopes there will be, and lives on the basis of that hope. Unable, in fact, to give empirical evidence of the worth and purpose of his own existence, he nonetheless works as if he has both. As he has repeatedly emphasized, faith cannot be a matter of absolute proof. Browning's speakers express this contingency in various ways. Bishop Blougram speaks for the believer in calling it "The grand Perhaps!" and argues that "it's best believing."

He is quite aware that, in agreeing to debate Gigadibs on Gigadib's own terms (agnosticism at least, if not disbelief), he is not departing very far from his own position. As this-worldly as Karshish or Cleon (or Sludge or the bishop of St. Praxed's), he is more pragmatic than they. He knows what he needs:

> I know the special kind of life I like,
> What suits the most my idiosyncrasy,
> Brings out the best of me and bears me fruit
> In power, peace, pleasantness and length of days.
> I find that positive belief does this
> For me, and unbelief, no whit of this.
>
> [234–239]

So he chooses belief. But his faith is a contingent one. He still must live "as if":

> You call for faith:
> I show you doubt, to prove that faith exists.
> The more of doubt, the stronger faith, I say,
> If faith o'ercomes doubt. How I know it does?
> By life and man's free will, God gave for that!
> To mould life as we choose it, shows our choice:
> That's our one act, the previous work's his own.
>
> [601–607]

The bishop's starting point is the same as Browning's: as a man, he is free to choose. For Blougram, the choice is God. As the succeeding lines demonstrate, it is a choice fraught with doubts both trivial and profound. Man cannot escape uncertainties in either belief or disbelief. Cleon and Karshish live as if the empirical system, accepting only verifiable physical evidence, has eliminated doubt. It has not done so; it has only eliminated man. Bishop Blougram, more sophisticated than they, knows his faith is hardly more certain than Gigadib's disbelief, but it is the only way for him. Furthermore, it meets the pragmatic test: it works.

This contingent and pragmatic approach to religion, so characteristic of Browning's monologuists, has led some of his critics to believe Browning to be strictly a relativist or pluralist in religion, keeping company with men like that famous student of religious experience, William James. This opinion is not far from the truth. The conclusion of Jame's great study, *Varieties of Religious Experience,* sounds like a summary of the experimental aspects of Browning's faith:

> Summing up in the broadest possible way the characteristics of the religious life, as we have found them, it includes the following beliefs:
>
> 1. That the visible world is part of a more spiritual universe from which it draws its chief significance;
>
> 2. That union or harmonious relation with that higher universe is our true end;
>
> 3. That prayer or inner communion with the spirit thereof—be that spirit "God" or "law"—is a process wherein work is really done, and spiritual energy flows in and produces effects, psychological or material, within the phenomenal world.
>
> Religion includes also the following psychological characteristics:
>
> 4. A new zest which adds itself like a gift to life, and takes the form either of lyrical enchantment or of appeal to earnestness and heroism.
>
> 5. An assurance of safety and a temper of peace, and, in relation to others, a preponderance of loving affections.[21]

James's method is more scientific than Browning's, but his conclusions are the same. James studied believers to see how they believed. Browning, as has been noted, studied himself, always beginning deep within his own experience to see how he believed, then objectifying his faith's various elements in his speakers. He is experimental insofar as he wishes to study how various concepts of God work for different persons. He is a relativist insofar as he believes that each person apprehends God according to his temperament, training, environment, and need. He is a pluralist in admitting that "on the earth the broken arcs" prevail and men must do the best they can to employ emotion, intelligence, and intuition to find the truth by combining the arcs; he is an absolutist in believing that there is, in fact, "in the heaven, a perfect round."[22] His wide reading and travel had convinced him of the relativity of forms of worship and systems of theology; his personal intuitions had convinced him to believe that there remains, above all, a unity. From the data of this world he moved to a belief in another world.

21. *Varieties of Religious Experience,* pp. 475–476.
22. *Abt Vogler,* IX, 8.

Browning's experimental method and existential posture, which have been the concerns of these two chapters, were given their most elaborate expression in his *magnum opus, The Ring and the Book,* a huge 21,116-line poem published in 1868–69. A retelling of a seventeenth-century murder story, this unlikely sensationalist thriller really serves as a vehicle for conveying dramatically (and exhaustively) Browning's mature epistemological, psychological, theological, anthropological, and moral reflections. His reliance upon a dramatic mode to expound his diverse views reflects his conviction that all these divisions of human thought are arbitrary and unnatural. Although for convenience men may speak of their minds or emotions or social or physical selves, they cannot really separate these aspects of themselves. They bring to each event in their lives their total persons, so that a single event will be experienced in a variety of ways by the various participants. This simple fact is the basis of *The Ring and the Book,* a single story told by ten speakers, each offering his version of the event. Each brings his experience, feelings, intellectual capacity, moral standards, and social standing—his total person—to the facts of the case. Each filters these facts through his personality. Because of the differences in the filters, the versions told by the speakers differ widely. Every speaker, in an attempt to tell the truth, can offer no more than an approximation of the truth; total objectivity is impossible. The complete truth eludes every human effort to capture it. In spite of the elusiveness of truth and the distortions caused by human personality, the poem demonstrates that every effort must be made to transcend all obstacles to apprehend the truth. Browning is not a complete skeptic. As painfully aware of man's limitations as he is, he does not lapse into intellectual lethargy or total distrust of men's intellectual powers.

The entire method of *The Ring and the Book* refutes those critics who condemn Browning for stigmatizing human knowledge. Carefully, systematically, Browning researched his subject, and just as meticulously he presented every possible view of the case. He found the story accidentally on a June day in 1860. He was rummaging around the Piazza San Lorenzo when in a book stall he found what has become famous as his *Old Yellow Book,* containing the history of

A Roman murder-case:
Position of the entire criminal cause
Of Guido Franceschini, nobleman,

With certain Four the cutthroats in his pay,
Tried, all five, and found guilty and put to death
By heading or hanging as befitted ranks, ·
At Rome on February Twenty-Two,
Since our salvation sixteen Ninety-Eight
Wherein it is disputed if, and when,
Husbands may kill adulterous wives, yet 'scape
The customary forfeit.

[I. 121–131]

Inside the book, he found the pleadings and counterpleadings, the testimonies of witnesses, and depositions of the defendants, and several other documents. Devouring its contents on his walk home, he could boast when he arrived at the Casa Guidi that he "had mastered the contents, knew the whole truth / Gathered together, bound up in his book" (I. 117–118). But was the truth bound up in the book the whole truth?

Was this truth of force?

Able to take its own part as truth should,
Sufficient, self-sustaining?

[I. 372–374]

The answer was no. For one reason, the *Old Yellow Book* was not the only record of the trial. So he took the book to Rome to investigate further; he also checked the annals of Arezzo. In 1862, he wrote to his good friend Isa Blagden to request that she obtain "M.S. account of the trial of Count Francesco Guidi for the murder of his wife,—which I am anxious to collate with my own collection of papers on the subject,"[23] which she sent and he studied thoroughly. In addition to his research and multiple readings of his sources, he brooded over the implications of the story for eight years before it was first published in 1868, and for four years before he actually began writing. Browning had to satisfy self-imposed standards of scholarship and his era's insistence on scientific factuality. He searched for every clue to corroborate the *Old Yellow Book's* documents. Additional documents found in this century show Browning to have been in error in some facts because of his close dependency for details upon his primary source, but these errors only substantiate his claims to fidelity to the known facts. This meticulous attention to his sources convinced Browning that

---

23. Browning to Isa Blagden, from Ste. Marie, September 19. *Dearest Isa*, p. 124.

the whole truth had not yet been heard. The contradictions, charges and countercharges, piling up of conflicting evidence, the possibilities of fraud, the complications of the legal system—where in the midst of this confusion lay the truth? Three hundred and seventeen times he used the word *truth* or *true* in this poem[24]—sometimes ironically, sometimes cynically, often desperately, reflecting Browning's struggle to find the truth. If he is later driven from research to intuition, it is because through thinking he has despaired of thought.

Yet thought can never be abandoned. Even the Pope, who sees with Browning the chaos of the case, must still take all the evidence fully into account before he can reach into himself for the verdict. The bewildering testimonies before him have to be weighed for the varying amount of truth in them. Only by multiplying points of view, Browning seems to say, can one then finally transcend one's viewpoint to glimpse more of the truth. Insofar as Browning allows each character his moment to expose his own portion of the facts, Browning is a relativist. But he never allows the reader to forget that there is fact which transcends point of view. Truth may be apprehended relative to one's context—but truth itself cannot ever be reduced entirely to one person's apprehension. At the core of *The Ring and the Book* is an event, a real murder by real men. Out of this empirical fact the poem arises.

The inaccessibility of the fact to readers two hundred years later, and the incompleteness of the understanding of each witness to and participant in the event do not make the murder any less a fact. In our time, President John F. Kennedy was assassinated in Dallas, Texas. His successor appointed an investigating commission headed by the Chief Justice of the Supreme Court to examine all the evidence of the case, checking every rumor and every possible explanation. Some men were convinced that there was an international conspiracy, others that Lee Oswald had several accomplices, others that he worked alone—and on and on went the speculation. The Warren Commission drew its own conclusions, filed its report, its findings were published, and the case was closed. Or was it? Ten years later, many Americans, including the president who appointed the commission, believe that all the truth has not been heard—and may never be. We have proved in our own experience what Browning proves in *The Ring and the Book*. We know, as Browning knew, that there was a murder. We

24. According to Richard Daniel Altick and James F. Loucks, II, *Browning's Roman Murder Story: A Reading of "The Ring and the Book,"* p. 121.

know several irrefutable facts about the murder—where and when it happened and to whom, the actual murderer, the consequences. We do not know the motives of all the participants; we can never know their relative guilt or innocence. Our approach must be that of Browning, who worked like a nineteenth-century scientist, checking all the evidence, running test after test to prove his hypotheses—then finally switching the standards of admissible evidence from empirical facts to the intuitions of the investigator.

In the first book, Browning states clearly that he values his Roman murder story both in itself and as an allegory of man's apprehension of the truth. Always interested in the grotesque, Browning relishes the sordid story and its diverse cast of characters, who belong in the company of Mr. Sludge, Rabbi ben Ezra, St. John, Fra Lippo Lippi, Colombe, and many others. The abiding significance of the event and the characters, however, is in the allegory, as Browning explains:

> Do you tell the story, now, in off-hand style,
> Straight from the book? Or simply here and there,
> (The while you vault it through the loose and large)
> Hang to a hint? Or is there book at all,
> And don't you deal in poetry, make-believe,
> And the white lies it sounds like?
>   Yes and no!
> From the book, yes; thence bit by bit I dug
> The lingot truth, that memorable day,
> Assayed and knew my piecemeal gain was gold—
> Yes; but from something else surpassing that,
> Something of mine which, mixed up with the mass,
> Made it bear hammer and be firm to file.
> Fancy with fact is just one fact the more;
> To-wit, that fancy has informed, transpierced,
> Thridded and so thrown fast the facts else free,
> As right through ring and ring runs the djereed
> And binds the loose, one bar without a break
> I fused my life soul and that inert stuff.
>
>   [I. 451–469]

The poem, which Browning calls a fusion of his "life soul and that inert stuff," symbolizes men's limited ability to ascertain complete empirical truth and his nearly unlimited capacity for blending fact and fancy into a higher form of truth. Each of the speakers relates

121

to the murder event as Browning relates to it: he is both observer and participant, even though he observes it from a distance of two hundred years. Each speaker within the poem, including the poet, relates his version of the tragedy, assuring his auditors that he speaks the truth, but so mixing the facts with his moral judgments and personal biases that the unalloyed truth cannot be found. The three anonymous commentators who did not participate personally in any way in the central events (Half-Rome, The Other Half-Rome, and Tertium Quid) cannot be any more objective than the actors themselves, for they participate vicariously in the event as they tell their story. Half-Rome, unhappily married to a termagant, adopts Guido's viewpoint, identifying sympathetically with Guido's wife-troubles. The Other Half-Rome, on the other hand, a bachelor with an eye for beauty and an appreciation for moral worth, readily believes in and defends the goodness of Pompilia. Tertium-Quid, as his name indicates, is a judicious person, a nobleman with more than a touch of aristocratic cynicism. His apparently detached review of the legal questions in the case and his unjudicious scorn of bourgeois life, in addition to his fawning attention to his audience, betray the speaker's interest in the case as little more than a means of ingratiating himself into Her Excellency's favor. Guido, Caponsacchi, and Pompilia all protest their innocence. Their "special-pleadings," as Donald Smalley calls them, manipulate the facts to justify their actions. Browning does not hesitate to identify Guido as the culprit for the reader, and to exonerate the hero and heroine—but in spite of Browning's partisanship and their marvelous defenses, the unalloyed truth still eludes us. The legal arguments prepared by the lawyers further compound the confusion. Undoubtedly Browning is caricaturing judicial proceedings in order to provide comic relief and to expose the injustices of legalism—goals which he supremely fulfills. The garrulous, doting, epicurean, Bible-misquoting Archangelis who defends Guido, and the equivocating, thoroughly professional, unsympathetic Bottinius play with words and lives with frightful detachment. The trial is just another sordid entry on their judicial calendars. Their concerns are legal, not moral or spiritual or personal. The truth does not matter; winning the case for their clients does. If the truth is lost in the subjective involvement of the earlier speakers, it is equally hidden in the supposed objectivity of the lawyer's detachment.

While writing *The Ring and the Book,* Browning must have turned with relief and eagerness from the lawyers to the Pope. Browning's restraint in allowing both lawyers to present their cases is remarkable, especially in light of Browning's—and the Pope's—thoroughly nonjudicial but warmly human and existential approach to truth. The Pope assumes a familiar posture among Browning's monologuists. He must make a life-and-death decision. Guido's fate hangs in the balance. Somehow Pope Innocent must pierce the hundreds of pages of testimony (as Browning has had to pierce the documents of the murder case) to find the truth buried somewhere at their center. And he must do this alone. He is isolated. As a judge, no one shares his responsibility:

> And I am bound, the solitary judge,
> To weigh the worth, decide upon the plea,
> And either hold a hand out, or withdraw
> A foot and let the wretch drift to the fall.
>
> [X. 194–197]

He cannot trust the transcripts of the legal case before him. The truth is there, but not in the words of testimony or in the lawyers' arguments:

> Truth, nowhere, lies yet everywhere in these—
> Not absolutely in a portion, yet
> Evolvible from the whole: evolved at last
> Painfully, held tenaciously by me.
>
> [X. 229–232]

He cannot find truth in the precedents of his ecclesiastical office. His review of the history of the papacy reveals only the fallibility, certainly not the inerrancy of the papal office. His predecessors cannot help him. Human intelligence cannot help him. He holds the briefs of highly intelligent persons: lawyers who will bend the truth to win a case, a priest, a nobleman, a virtuous young woman, all of whom will consciously or unconsciously deflect the truth to justify their behavior. Without trustworthy precedent, accurate facts, supporting colleagues, or sufficient intelligence, the Pope still with "uncertain hand" must make his decision. In a very real sense, the Pope is Browning's Everyman, the symbol of all men who, in the crises of life, cannot escape the responsibility to choose their own way. The Pope is not only Christ's representative; he is also man's.

In his discursive review of the case, the Pope touches upon all of Browning's familiar doctrines. These indicate the tenacity with which Browning has retained beliefs which he first evidences in

Pauline, and will show that there is no doubt that the Pope speaks for Browning. He begins in the full consciousness of man's limitations:

> "God who set me to judge thee, meted out
> So much of judging faculty, no more."
>
> [X. 265–266]

In contrast to man's finitude is God's infinitude:

> O Thou,—as represented here to me
> In such conception as my soul allows,—
> Under Thy measureless, my atom width!—
>
> [X. 1308–1310]

Since man's mind cannot grasp the full reality of God, and man's senses are sometimes weak and deceptive, he cannot trust either exclusively. He must, instead, accept himself fully, realizing the superiority of the soul to any single aspect of his being. That soul is best exemplified, the Pope believes, in the purity of Pompilia:

> Everywhere
> I see in the world the intellect of man,
> That sword, the energy his subtle spear,
> The knowledge which defends him like a shield—
> Everywhere; but they make not up, I think,
> The marvel of a soul like thine, earth's flower
> She holds up to the softened gaze of God!
>
> [X. 1013–1019]

Although he is so much aware of a human weakness and limitation, the Pope refuses to grant man's earthly existence as his only one. For the Pope, life is but the beginning:

> Life is probation and the earth no goal
> But starting-point of man: compel him strive,
> Which means, in man, as good as reach the goal.
>
> [X. 1436–1438]

Temptation and struggle are essential for man's growth; they define him as man:

> Why comes temptation but for man to meet
> And master and make crouch beneath his foot,
> And so be pedestaled in triumph?
>
> [X. 1185–1187]

In the midst of his struggle, his overriding need is for love. Thus, for the Pope, as for Karshish, the speakers of *Christmas-Eve and Easter-Day,* David, and so many other Browning characters, love is the necessary characteristic of God:

> Conjecture of the worker by the work:
> Is there strength there?—enough: intelligence?
> Ample: but goodness in a like degree?
> Not to the human eye in the present state,
> An isoscele deficient in the base.
> What lacks, then, of perfection fit for God
> But just the instance which this tale supplies
> Of love without a limit? So is strength,
> So is intelligence; let love be so,
> Unlimited in its self-sacrifice,
> Then is the tale true and God shows complete
>
>   [X. 1362–1372]

If Love is God, then one can accept the uncertainty of knowledge and the inescapable doubt within faith. In fact, faith which includes doubt is to be preferred to that which denies it:

> Unless . . . what whispers me of times to come?
> What if it be the mission of that age
> My death will usher into life, to shake
> This torpor of assurance from our creed,
> Re-introduce the doubt discarded, bring
> That formidable danger back, we drove
> Long ago to the distance and the dark?
>
>   [X. 1851–1857]

In spite of the inadequacy of knowledge, one still must choose one's own way, relying upon intuition and the fragmentary information he has:

>   Thus, bold
> Yet self-mistrusting, should man bear himself,
> Most assured on what now concern him most—
> The law of his own life, the path he prints—
> Which law is virtue and not vice, I say.
>
>   [X. 1753–1757]

One must choose: "Life's business being just the terrible choice." The one certainty the Pope knows, stronger even than the talk of God's sacrifice of love, is his own feelings:

> Beyond the tale, I reach into the dark,
> Feel what I cannot see, and still faith stands:
> I can believe this dread machinery
> Of sin and sorrow would confound me else.
>
> [X. 1373–1376]

The Pope couples this reliance upon feeling with Browning's customary moral concern. Sin and sorrow were

> Devised,—all pain, at most expenditure
> Of pain by Who devised pain,—to evolve,
> By new machinery in counterpart,
> The moral qualities of man—how else?—
> To make him love in turn and be beloved,
> Creative and self-sacrificing too,
> And thus eventually God-like, (ay
> "I have said ye are Gods," —shall it be said for nought?)
> Enable man to wring, from out all pain,
> All pleasure for a common heritage
> To all eternity.
>
> [X. 1377–1387]

Through pain and evil men evolve morally and spiritually toward eternity. This fact, says Browning, can be surmised from man's nature. The nature of Divine Love, however, cannot be so derived; it is known only in the crucifixion, in which Love received its fullest consummation. Even this revelation of Love, though, can be accepted only in faith, for it, too, defies final empirical verification:

> Whether a fact,
> Absolute, abstract, independent truth,
> Historic, not reduced to suit man's mind,—
> Or only truth reverberate, changed, made pass
> A spectrum into mind, the narrow eye,—
> The same and not the same, else unconceived—
> Though quite conceivable to the next grade
> Above it in intelligence.
>
> [X. 1388–1395]

This disregard for the historicity of the crucifixion re-emphasizes Browning's existential pragmatism. Because it works—that is, because the tale of the crucifixion meets the soul's demand for some indication of limitless love as well as power and intelligence, an indication which cannot be found in either physical or human nature—he chooses to believe it. In repeating this familiar formula of Browning's, the Pope joins the less famous Dissenter of *Christmas-Eve* and all the other religious spokesmen of Browning, in basing his faith completely upon his own authority and not at all upon ecclesiastical tradition or dogma. As Browning was aware, when he first found *The Old Yellow Book,* that the book contained truth but not the whole truth, so the Pope knows that all the records of the murder case contained some—but not all—the truth. The higher truth upon which human life can be built and personal decisions can be based is approached only through the alloy of fact and fancy, the objective event and the subjective interpretation of the event.

We end where Browning always ends. Truth does exist independent of the observer, but it can never be apprehended in its purity upon this earth. In spite of every effort to appear objective, every man fuses his "life soul and that inert stuff" called fact. Although the experimental method is invaluable as a means for pragmatically testing and justifying one's faith, it cannot lead anyone to total certainty about God or man's relation to Him. Belief in God remains a matter of choice, not compulsion. Browning believes because he trusts the impulses of his inner being, just as the Pope must trust his intuition in pronouncing his judgments. Having examined every portion of the evidence, he still must step beyond fact into faith.

The Meaning of God

The basic question concerning Robert Browning's faith remains unanswered: "When Browning says *God,* what does he mean?" As we have seen, the subjective autonomy with which Browning approaches all ultimate questions places him among nineteenth- and twentieth-century existentialists, for whom *God* has no single, objective referent. The term *existentialist* cannot satisfactorily account for his faith, however. Although his method of thinking was existential, Browning did not accept the conclusions to which consistent subjectivity often leads: radical individualism, inherently meaningless life, relativity of truth, absurdity of existence. He was more Cartesian than existential, in that his subjectivity led him to God, not away from Him. Agreeing with Descartes in trusting knowledge of oneself above any other kind of knowledge, he likewise believed that self-knowledge leads to a knowledge of God sufficient to engender belief in Him. He stopped short of identifying truth with intuition, or of measuring accuracy of choice by the earnestness of the decision. Sharing Sören Kierkegaard's respect for individual choice, he nonetheless would have had to reject the Danish existentialist's opinion that "in making a choice it is not so much a question of choosing the right as of the energy, the earnestness, the pathos with which one chooses."[1] For Browning, there is a right to be chosen; there is a God above. He did not believe in belief; he believed in God. The word *God,* obscured as it is with personal and cultural connotations, nevertheless has meaning for him. It points to a reality beyond the finite, a Being

1. *Either/or,* translated by Walter Lowrie. In *The Modern Tradition: Backgrounds of Modern Literature,* edited by Richard Ellman and Charles Feidelson, Jr., p. 830.

of whom men can catch occasional and indefinite glimpses, One who calls men to Himself.

Although Robert Browning's letters speak very seldom in any detail about religious matters, they often allude to God in personal comments. He speaks to Elizabeth Barrett of his determination to risk everything for love, "trusting to God for protection here or recompense hereafter."[2] He promises to "preserve this love . . . for which I trust to God who procured it for me, and doubtlessly can preserve it."[3] He will provide proof of his affection, "such a perfect proof" which he will endeavour "with God's help."[4] He speaks confidently of his knowledge of God's will for Elizabeth: "I *do* say—were the best blessing of all, the blessing I trust and believe God intends, of your perfect restoration to health."[5] He recognizes God's providence in his coming union with Miss Barrett: "My own Ba! My election is made or God made it for me—and is irrevocable."[6] He does not hesitate to come to God's defense with his own mind: "I do dare say, for the justification of God, who gave the mind to be *used* in this world,—where it saves us, we are taught, or destroys us."[7] Early in their correspondence he writes, in a favorite expression of his, of his relationship with God: "You will never drop *me* off the golden hooks, I dare believe—and the rest is with God—whose finger I see every minute of my life."[8] In 1849, he sent Miss Mary Russell the happy news that he and "Ba" were parents of "a fine, strong boy." "Now all is over," he reports, "the babe seems happy in his cradle, and Ba *is*, I suppose, the very thing you call happy—this is God's reward for her entire perfectness to me and everybody but herself."[9]

The God who rewards also takes away. A few years later, in 1861, he had to reconcile himself to Mrs. Browning's death. To do so, he found comfort in belief in God. To his sister Sarianna Browning he wrote, "She is with God, who takes from me the life of my life in one sense,—not so, in the truest. My life is fixed and sure now.

2. Browning to Elizabeth Barrett, September 4, 1846. *The Letters of Robert Browning and Elizabeth Barrett Browning,* edited by Robert Barrett Browning, II, pp. 517–518.

3. September 12, 1846. *Ibid.,* II, p. 540.

4. September 14, 1846. *Ibid.,* II, p. 545.

5. March 26, 1846. *Ibid.,* II, p. 7.

6. April 10, 1846. *Ibid.,* II, p. 58.

7. March 3, 1846. *Ibid.,* I, p. 530.

8. No date. *Ibid.,* I, p. 133.

9. Browning to Mary Russell, March 9, 1849. *Letters of Robert Browning Collected by Thomas J. Wise,* edited by Thurman L. Hood, p. 22.

I shall live out the remainder in her direct influence, endeavoring to complete mine, miserably imperfect now, but so as to take the good she was meant to give me."[10] A month later, he sent another letter, the mood less serene: "What I lose is another thing. And for Pen, it can't be helped—a woman ought to be center of a home, but God has not allowed it here."[11] He spoke these words of the woman to whom he frequently sent prayers as salutations: "May God requite you, my best beloved," or "May God keep you at all times, ever dearest!"[12]

Throughout his correspondence with Elizabeth Barrett, and later with his sister, with Isa Blagden, and to some extent with Julia Wedgwood, Browning frequently employs God's name, alluding to God in order to emphasize his affection, or to account for an inexplicable or undesirable event such as "Ba's" death, or to assert purposefulness in his life and goals, or even to sanctify his opinions.[13] He usually sounds like a pious Christian, but he does not scruple to employ more literary terms, as in a letter to Miss Isa Blagden: "I think it will not be Florence I return to, however,—except for a day or two: all which lies on the knees of the Gods, as Homer says."[14] Whether he refers to God or the Gods, he consistently conceives of the divine as beyond the boundaries of human thought and endeavor. In another letter to Miss Blagden, comforting her upon the death of Louisa Alexander, whom she nursed, he simply states what he elsewhere discusses at great length: "What you could not do for her, God has done."[15] Where human effort fails, divine power prevails, Browning steadfastly believed. Conscious always of human fallibility, Browning

10. June 30, 1861. *Ibid.*, p. 62.

11. July 22, 1861. *New Letters of Robert Browning*, edited by William Clyde deVane and Kenneth Leslie Knickerbocker, p. 141.

12. *Letters of Robert Browning and Elizabeth Barrett Browning*, II, pp. 131, 343.

13. A comparison of Browning's correspondence with his men and his women friends is suggestive. In writing to the women, Browning often uses God-language and sometimes discusses religion. With men, however, he is more reticent. In letters to Alfred Domett, he confines himself to two references to chapel attendance. In writing to the Storys, he says "God bless you" twice when addressing both Mr. and Mrs. Story, but he never uses God-language with Mr. Story alone. His letters to men are notable for their lack of religious language. See *Browning to His American Friends: Letters between the Brownings, the Storys and James Russell, 1841–1890*, edited by Gertrude Reese Hudson; and *Robert Browning and Alfred Domett*, edited by Frederic G. Kenyon.

14. October 19, 1868. *Dearest Isa: Robert Browning's Letters to Isabella Blagden*, edited by Edward C. McAleer, p. 301.

15. October 2, 1858. *Ibid.*, p. 21.

could not believe that the power governing the universe could be similarly limited. In his thinking, man's limitedness implies the Unlimited. Man's reaching outward demands that there be Something or Someone beyond to receive him. God is the One who takes over after men have expended all their energies to reach Him, as Browning explained to his friend Julia Wedgwood:

> There is lightness in this, because if you take my arm you must keep my pace, and HOPE: do you know, a phrenologist told me when I was about sixteen that I had absolutely no hope at all in the head of me—and so it really was in those days. But I do think I see light at the far end of the passage. Not that I should like you at all to stand in my place so far from the entry: you should *live,* step by step, up to the proper place where the pin-point of light is visible: nothing is to be over-leaped, the joy no more than the sorrow, and then, your part done, God's may follow, and will, I trust.[16]

Browning's casual employment of the term *God* as controller of his actions in several of his letters and poems seems inconsistent with his usual emphasis upon individual freedom. There is no way to reconcile Browning's professed belief in God's determination of his affairs with his many testimonies to his trust in human freedom, if all his references to God are to be read literally. If everything "lies on the knees of the Gods," then men are free only insofar as the Gods allow, which is not real freedom at all. This inconsistency in Browning's thinking was never resolved. In fact, in spite of his continued wrestling with problems of good and evil, of knowledge and nescience, of freedom and determinism, and of finitude and infinitude, Browning could never satisfy himself in terms of this world. Thus the persistent determination of Paracelsus to know all truth becomes, in time, Ferishtah's stoical acceptance of inevitable ignorance. Ferishtah knows nothing "save that love I can / Boundlessly, endlessly." The strain of epistemological skepticism which begins in Browning's earliest poems runs through his latest. Man cannot know all he would like. Even worse, perhaps, he cannot express all that he knows. Pauline's poet cries out that "words are wild and weak" and cannot express his love. Sordello finds that

---

16. June 27, 1864. *Robert Browning and Julia Wedgwood: A Broken Friendship as Revealed by Their Letters,* edited by Richard Curle, p. 15.

          perceptions whole, like that he sought
To clothe, reject so pure a work of thought
As language.

                                        [II. 589–591]

Problems which must be solved in human language will remain
unsolved. In his helplessness to account for life's experiences in terms
of earthly existence and human vocabulary, Browning must turn to
a world beyond this one and to communication which is more concrete
and immediate than written or spoken words. Only in a future existence can earthly puzzles be solved; only in immediate individual
experience can earthly joy be found.

   Often justly criticized for imprecision and redundancy in his word
usage, Browning may be partially vindicated, at least, by pointing
to his attempts to compensate for the weakness of words through
employing other media. He praised and used music, for example,
for its direct appeal to the emotions and its superiority to words:

   Ah, Music, wouldst thou help! Words struggle with the weight
   So feebly of the False, thick element between
   Our soul, the True, and Truth! which, but that intervene
   False shows of things, were reached as easily by thought
   Reducible to word, as now by yearnings wrought
   Up with thy fine free force, oh Music, that canst thrid,
   Electrically win a passage through the lid
   Of earthly sepulchre, our words may push against,
   Hardly transpierce as thou![17]

Music can reach to heaven, soaring beyond the potential of human
language. Art is another medium which can overcome the weakness
of words:

   Why take the artistic way to prove so much?
   Because, it is the glory and good of Art,
   That Art remains the one way possible
   Of speaking truth, to mouths like mine at least . . .
   But Art,—wherein man nowise speaks to men,
   Only to mankind,—Art may tell a truth
   Obliquely, do the thing shall breed the thought,
   Nor wrong the thought, missing the mediate word.[18]

17. *Fifine at the Fair*, pp. 943–955, 960–963.
18. *The Ring and the Book*, XII, 835–844, 858–867.

Browning's most important substitute for human language, more significant than either music or art in his work, is dramatization. In his dramatic monologues at their best, thought is embodied in action. Words are inseparable from deeds, faith inextricably one with works. Statements derive their meaning from a life in action. Thus *God* does not mean the same when Johannes Agricola uses it as it does in the deliberations of Pope Innocent. If music can transcend the limits of human language, and art can tell a truth as truth can only be told, obliquely—then dramatization can capture the variety and individuality of personal apprehension of and relation to truth. A character's use of God-language may refer indirectly to the doctrines of a religious tradition, but it directly reveals the speaker's values and aspirations. Throughout Browning's several religious poems one senses that the poet is really not concerned with any serious attempt to systematize a theology or resolve any philosophical dilemmas. Epistemological questions will be settled, if at all, in a life beyond this one. What one can study now, Browning seems to suggest concerning religious questions, is the multivalence of religious language as it becomes colored by the experiences of its several speakers. Because language can never become abstracted from human experience, it is always subject to modification by each speaker; hence it can never achieve precision. Limited by the powers of human cognition and by the individual intentions of its various speakers, all language—including religious language—can never do more than approximate the truth.

Browning's awareness of the deficiencies of language becomes almost painfully obvious to the reader when the poet attempts to express beliefs which are fundamental to everything else. He bases his entire philosophy of life upon his assurance that the soul exists—but he finds it impossible to say what he means by *soul*:

> "Soul"—(accept
> A word which vaguely names what no adept
> In word-use fits and fixes so that still
> Thing shall not slip word's fetter and remain
> Innominate as first, yet, free again,
> Is no less recognized the absolute
> Fact underlying that same other fact
> Concerning which no cavil can dispute
> Our nomenclature when we call it "Mind"—

Something not Matter)—"Soul," who seeks shall find
Distinct beneath that something.[19]

The meaning of *soul* cannot adequately be conveyed by any denomination—yet the reality underlying the vague and slippery term *soul* remains. Therefore some term, he says, however insufficient, is necessary to acknowledge the existence of this reality which so completely transcends the power of vocabulary to express it. The soul is mind, but more than mind; it is intelligence, emotion, spirituality, life-force, intuition and more, all in one. Being "above and *behind* the intellect which is merely its servant,"[20] the soul defies any definition to capture its essence, for all definitions are products of inferior intellect. Thus *soul* does not define soul; it merely points to it.

In the same way, *God* cannot define God; it can only acknowledge the existence of an ineffable Being who is known by faith alone. Prince Hohenstiel-Schwangau employs a familiar Browning argument for God, displaying Browning's recognition of words as convenient but imprecise tools:

> I recognize
> Power passing mine, immeasurable, God—
> Above me, whom He made, as heaven beyond
> Earth—to use figures which assist our sense.
> I know that He is there as I am here,
> By the same proof, which seems no proof at all,
> It so exceeds familiar forms of proof.
> Why "there," not "here"? Because, when I say "there,"
> I treat the feeling with distincter shape
> That space exists between us: I,—not He,—
> Live, think, do human work here—no machine,
> His will moves, but a being by myself,
> His, and not He who made me for a work,
> Watches my working, judges its effect,
> But does not interpose.
>
> [111–125]

---

19. "Charles Avison," *Parleyings with Certain People of Importance in Their Day,* pp. 139–150.

20. *Learned Lady: Letters from Robert Browning to Mrs. Thomas FitzGerald 1876-1889,* edited by Edward C. McAleer, p. 34. Later in the letter, Browning unconsciously limits *soul* and violates his own definition by calling it "religious feeling."

Religious terms, according to the Prince, are "figures which assist our sense." Not merely subjective projections, however; they point beyond the subjective to an objective reality. The difficulty with this religious language is that any attempt to capture the essence of reality in words is a distortion:

> Alack, one lies oneself
> Even in the stating that one's end was truth,
> Truth only, if one states as much in words!
> Give me the inner chamber of the soul
> For obvious easy argument! 'T is there
> One pits the silent truth against a lie.
>
> [2123–2128]

Fully cognizant of these tendencies of language to obscure or pervert meaning, Browning nevertheless employs God-language throughout his career. Unable to explain God's essence, he uses religious language to express psychological truth. He believes that human beings have depths (which he calls *soul* or *yearnings*) which a strict naturalism—whether it be Darwinian evolution, scientific mechanism, dialectical rationalism, or a variation of humanism—cannot satisfy. He agrees with Kant in focusing upon human benefits of God-language: "We are entitled . . . to suppose that transcendental ideas . . . have an excellent, and indeed indispensably necessary, regulative employment, namely, that of directing the understanding towards a certain goal upon which the routes marked out by all its rules converge, as upon their point of intersection."[21]

The speakers of Browning's monologues, and Browning himself in his more autobiographical poems, do not care about God as a metaphysical or cosmological principle. A God who is merely a First Cause or an Absolute Other or a Perfect Being is no God at all to the typical Browning speaker. Each speaks of his God in abstractions like Power or Mind, but He is a personal God, relating to each one and fulfilling his utmost desires. Martin Buber's definition of a "personal God" expresses Browning's understanding and that of his monologuists:

> The designation of God as a person is indispensable for all
> who, like myself, do not mean a principle when they say "God,"

---

21. Immanuel Kant, *Critique of Pure Reason*, translated by N. Kemp Smith. In W. T. Jones, *Kant to Wittgenstein and Sartre: A History of Western Philosophy*, second ed., p. 59.

135

although mystics like Eckhart occasionally equate "Being" with him, and who, like myself, do not mean an idea when they say "God," although philosophers like Plato could at times take him for one—all who, like myself, mean by "God" him that, whatever else he may be in addition, enters into a direct relationship to us human beings through creative, revelatory, and redemptive acts, and thus makes it possible for us to enter into a direct relationship to him. This ground and meaning of our existence establishes each time a mutuality of the kind that can obtain only between persons. The concept of personhood is, of course, utterly incapable of describing the nature of God; but it is permitted and necessary to say that God is *also* a person.[22]

Buber's analysis of the meaning of a personal God is an appropriate defense of Browning's use of the term. Unable to reduce the infinite God to finite language, Browning adopts traditional religious vocabulary, with its anthropomorphic connotations, in order to express the universal human religious impulses to experience a relationship with transcendental reality. He is not only aware that his religious terms lack specificity of reference; he is also aware that denotative precision is not desired by most users of religious language. God-language expresses relation, aspiration, self-identification. As popularly used, it has little representational function. Browning does not deny that religious language is often historically based; he makes frequent reference to the Christ-event, and to certain Old and New Testament personalities and events. Nonetheless, when he moves from history to supramundane reality, for which there is no given vocabulary, he finds justification for faith in the supernatural only by reference to the psychological effects of belief. Thus he asserts that God is Love, because he has found the personal relationship called love the most profound and satisfying human experience. This experience, he concludes, is the key to universal reality. But as *love* is a weak symbol of a powerful relationship, so *God* is a woefully inadequate symbol of the entire family of concepts which personally and culturally adhere to it. The word reveals nothing whatsoever about that to which it points. The use of the word, however, is an irreplaceable indication of the personality and character of the user. In many of Browning's poems, God-language is little else. The speakers assume that God is; they do not venture to define Him

22. *I and Thou*, translated by Walter Kaufman, pp. 180-181.

metaphysically. Rather, they identify Him as their personal God and assume their characteristics to be His. In speaking about God, they reveal themselves.

Browning's typical use of theological language to reveal character has been brilliantly delineated by Park Honan in a study of the word *God* in *The Bishop Orders His Tomb at St. Praxed's*. Noting that the Bishop says "God" seven times, each time with a somewhat different meaning, Honan discusses these several applications of the word. One *God* is "a special kind of interjection" which "reflects the Bishop's awareness of incongruity between his ecclesiastical office and commitments on the one hand, and on the other his own past behavior which has produced 'sons.'" Another time, *God* becomes "simply a convenient supernatural medium through which he may strike a last blow at his rival." In the third instance, the word reflects "the Bishop's awareness of incongruity between his role as Bishop," a traditional office which he fills in the present, and his "sons," a sin of the past which continues to involve him in "a new, venial sin, even as he speaks." In the fourth instance, the term "is merely an expression of his ardor with respect to the *lapis*"; and, in the fifth, *God* "is the Almighty Maker of the world and Father of all mankind." Later, *God* becomes "the Christ of transubstantiation"; and, finally, "*God* becomes equivalent merely to an expression of degree, a way of saying that he knows his sons' wish for his death is a particularly intense one." Thus, as Honan summarizes, "*God* is not only the maker of the world and Father of man, as well as Christ, but a convenient weapon against a rival, a means of mitigating if not avoiding altogether the implications of past and present sin, a justification of sensual ardor, and a handy implement of rhetoric."[23]

In Browning's letters and autobiographical poems, his application of God-language serves as conveniently as the Bishop of St. Praxed's to express his values. He regularly attributes human values to God. In fact, he insists that God conform to his standards. A God whose actions run counter to Browning's values of justice, love, mercy, and wisdom is no God at all. "I should never dare attribute to God," he writes to Mrs. FitzGerald, "what would be injustice in a human being—nay, in a *less* degree,—and think Him capable of punishing what Himself was the agent in producing. That is my opinion, and it is inexplicable to me how people with a belief in the Mercy and Rectitude of God can have any other. Trust in these, dear Friend,—and

23. Park Honan, *Browning's Characters: A Study in Poetic Technique*, pp. 218–219.

dismiss all such fancies as derogatory to the All-good and All-wise."[24] As noted in the first chapter, he once asked Elizabeth Barrett why men should "declare that 'the Lord *is* holy, just and good' unless there is recognized and independent conception of holiness and goodness, to which the subsequent assertion is referable? 'You know what *holiness* is, what it is to be good? Then, He *is* that'—not, '*that* is so—because *he* is that."[25] In Browning's references to God, as these letters make plain, he accomplishes two purposes: he acknowledges the existence of transcendent reality, which is so infinitely superior to human intelligence that it cannot be comprehended; and he projects his personal value system upon metaphysical reality, describing the indescribable in the language of human experience. In this sense, all of Browning's religious language is symbolic, explaining the unknown and unknowable by reference to the known. His frame of reference is always human. Browning would have accepted Tillich's understanding of *God* as symbol:

> God is the basic and universal symbol for what concerns us ultimately. As being-itself He is ultimate reality, the really real, the ground and abyss of everything that is real. As the God with whom I have a person-to-person encounter, He is the subject of all the symbolic statements in which I express my ultimate concern. Everything we say about being-itself, the ground and abyss of being, must be symbolic. It is taken out of the material of our finite reality and applied to that which transcends the finite infinitely. Therefore it cannot be used in its literal sense.[26]

Thus, Tillich adds, when we speak of God as love, "we use our experience of love and our analysis of life as the material which alone we can use." To speak of God as Power means "the feeling of being in the hand of a power which cannot be conquered by any other power, in ontological terms, which is the infinite resistance against non-being and the eternal victory over it."[27] To speak of God as Mind, as Paracelsus does, is to project our admiration for human intelligence into the divine realm, accepting as real the possibility

---

24. August 28, 1876. *Learned Lady*, p. 35.
25. January 14, 1846. *Letters of Robert Browning and Elizabeth Barrett Browning*, I, p. 415.
26. *Love, Power and Justice*, p. 109.
27. *Ibid.*, pp. 109–110.

that somewhere incomplete human intelligence exists as complete, divine omniscience.

Browning explicitly calls God Love, Power, and Mind in his poems and letters. But one of his most important concepts remains implicit: God as Future or Hope, the God who beckons all created reality onward. It is easy to overlook this vital understanding of God in Browning's works, because his existential faith so strongly emphasizes the here and now. He frequently stresses that moments of truth come when, in concrete events, the infinite enters the finite, revealing a glimpse of the limitless to persons bound to the physical. In *The Statue and the Bust*, in *Pippa Passes*, in *In a Balcony*, and in many other poems Browning reiterates his version of *carpe diem*: only in moments of action and decision can truth and love be found. Life—physical, sensuous, passionate, dynamic life—is to be enjoyed now. Life cannot be enslaved by traditions of a dead past, but must be experienced in the immediate present. However, for Browning, true joy cannot come to one from whom the present moment is divorced from a future toward which the present can move. The lesson of *Pauline*, the examples of Paracelsus and Sordello and the speaker in *Easter-Day*, the conversion of Caponsacchi from a mediocre canon to a knight of God, and even the perverted determination of Johannes Agricola who vowed "I intend to get to God," prove that the present has meaning only when it leans toward the future. The "here and now" is empty if it does not anticipate a "then and there" in which today's promises will be fulfilled. Beyond any doubt, Browning believed that the present moment is all a man has. He rejected both a romantic longing for some supposed "Golden Age" and a naive belief that all would be well in the "sweet by and by." But the past and the future are vital for their contribution to today.

Browning's profound sense of the future has misled many of his readers. No aspect of his faith has received more discussion than his famed optimism, which is but one element in his concept of God as Future. Readers who know almost nothing else about Browning can at least quote his famous lines from *Pippa Passes*:

> God's in his heaven—
> All's right with the world!

Many of his frequently anthologized poems—and his most quotable lines—contribute to his reputation as a supreme and somewhat naive optimist, one who can

welcome each rebuff
    That turns earth's smoothness rough,
  Each sting that bids nor sit nor stand but go![28]

While other existentialist writers have despaired of purpose and meaning in life, Browning has reassured his readers that

        This world's no blot for us,
  Nor blank; it means intensely, and means good:
  To find its meaning is my meat and drink.[29]

Even as a very old man, in the year of his death, he described himself as

  One who never turned his back but marched breast forward,
    Never doubted clouds would break,
  Never dreamed though right were worsted, wrong would triumph,
  Held we fall to rise, are baffled to fight better,
    Sleep to wake.[30]

His words fulfill the promise in the invitation of Rabbi ben Ezra:

  Grow old along with me!
  The best is yet to be,
The last of life, for which the first was made:
  Our times are in His hand
  Who saith "A whole I planned,
"Youth shows but half; trust God: see all nor be afraid!"

                                 [1–6]

The easy optimism expressed in these lines has led several critics to seek the source of such unusual ebullience. John Robertson found it in "an excellent constitution, a good income, a sense of having no duty to humanity that is not fulfilled by writing poems, a capacity for cosmopolitanism, tolerable insensibility to the woes of the world, and the capacity to fall in love when past seventy."[31] William Sharp summarizes his condition more succinctly: "It is difficult for a happy

28. *Rabbi Ben Ezra*, pp. 31–33.
29. *Fra Lippo Lippi*, pp. 313–315.
30. "Epilogue" to *Asolando*, pp. 9–12.
31. *Browning and Tennyson as Teachers*, p. 134.

man with an imperturbable digestion to be a pessimist."[32] Later writers, more conscious of Browning's complexity, have explained his optimism as a compensation for doubt and insecurity rather than as a natural expression of his physical constitution. Richard D. Altick, we noted earlier, accounts for Browning's robustness by describing it as a facade covering his psychological neuroses and his philosophical ineptitude. In religious issues, these personal weaknesses betrayed themselves in his refusal to debate "the powerful arguments of his adversaries." Instead, he

> insisted upon his own cherished principle of faith—the faith that men hold, intuitively, even mystically, the knowledge of God and His love which is impossible to anyone who relies upon the deceptive charms of reason. The more he became aware, as the years passed, of the swelling tide of rationalism and agnosticism, the more passionately he insisted that divinely granted intuition was the only means to truth. He could not live without that supreme assurance, and therefore much of his life was occupied in reiterating it, as if in an attempt at self-hypnosis: "I believe . . . I believe . . . I believe . . . of course I believe.[33]

Altick's explanation is as inadequate as Sharp's or Robertson's. They all deny to Browning any respect as a thinker. Optimism must be a matter of personality, not of principle, they insist.

Browning's less widely-known poems lead one to question the appropriateness of the term *optimist* as a description of Browning. Melancholy moods, vivid portrayals of human and natural evil, and repeated testimonials to man's weakness and helplessness are not usually the characteristic expressions of a naive optimist. For all their claims to victory, Browning's men and women are overwhelmingly defeated and defensive personalities. Even little Pippa, whose innocent song has been taken seriously as an aphoristic summary of Browning's creed, knew that "all's right with the world" for her holiday only. Before beginning her one-day vacation, she pleads with her special Day, hoping to find enough strength during the day to face another dreary year:

32. *Life of Robert Browning,* p. 24.
33. "The Private Life of Robert Browning," *Yale Review* XLI (December 1951), reprinted in *The Browning Critics,* edited by Boyd Litzinger and E. L. Knickerbocker, pp. 260–261.

For, Day, my holiday, if thou ill-usest
Me, who am only Pippa,—old-year's sorrow,
Cast off last night, will come again tomorrow:
Whereas, if thou prove gentle, I shall borrow
Sufficient strength of thee for new-year's sorrow.

[30–34]

Browning's masterpiece, *The Ring and the Book,* is a genuinely pessimistic document, demonstrating man's utter inability to know spiritual or temporal truth. Browning rejects such traditional depositories of human culture as orthodox religion, systematized law, rational liberalism, classical idealism, or any combination or modification of them. When speaking through the Pope, he turns to subjective apprehension of truth. He does so because everything else has failed. It is an act of desperation, not of optimism. Convinced that every traditional authority of man is untrustworthy, he has no one else to turn to but himself. This is not the approach of one who believes "all's right with the world."

It is evident that Browning's faith cannot be equated with the subjective optimism of many Romantic poets. In stressing self-reliance, he does not share Ralph Waldo Emerson's belief in the divinity of man. For Browning, religion is a learned rather than an inherent trait. There is no natural goodness in man which has somehow been obscured by this world's occupations. Primitive intuition cannot solve men's problems any more than systematic rationalism can. He does not share Wordsworth's belief in natural piety. Disagreeing with Wordsworth that the child is closer to reality than the man is, he affirms the opposite: adult man, recognizing his limitations in a way a child never does, reaches out for God with an intensity and desperation quite foreign to childhood. In a letter to Julia Wedgwood he explains his definitely nonromantic concept of the religious attitude:

> I observe nowhere in youth, except in diseased and dying youth, the religious instincts: religious dogmas are accepted at that age undoubtingly, but they don't influence a child's actions at all—that business is done by quite other agents: it is curious to observe what practical atheism, so far as regards the God themselves affect to believe in, distinguishes ordinary children: they have not a natural need for what you artificially give them, and so, without at all disputing your dogmas' truth, they never apply them in any difficulty, having better ways of their own for righting matters:

142

whereas the real instinct is developed with mature years, and, then only, substitutes itself for the previous motives which are losing their virtue of impelling or repressing one—hence the new birth: while this life suffices, I don't see that another incentive to push on through its insufficiency, in the shape of a conceived possibility of a life beyond, is never given us. I know that I possess at this minute every advantage that I had thirty-five years ago, even to the health and power of physical enjoyment—added to plenty of acquisition undreamed of at that time—and yet have outgrown all considerations which used to manage, for better and worse, the wise person of my perfect remembrance and particular dislike—but there are now finger posts in this far end of the road, as it once seemed, and I am less than ever my own master: that, however, is far from meaning that one is clearly another's servant,—life would not be what life *is*—and is, for a good reason probably,—if one or the other relation could be clearly determined,—one could then live forever:—it is because one cannot so live on now, under the present conditions, in virtue of the very desire to live in a conceivable absolute freedom and fulness of life,—that I hope this to be one day.[34]

Browning's faith is rooted in growth, not in natural piety. The themes of growth from physical to spiritual life, from a sense of insufficiency to a hope in eventual perfection, and from bondage to freedom inspire his religious poems. Starting in this letter, as he always does, with the nature of man—that is, the nature of Robert Browning—he expresses man's essential need to hope. He calls that hope "religious instinct." The religious man chooses an attitude of expectancy, wanting to believe that some day this world's boundaries can be crossed and that what is only potential on earth will become actual in the next life. Browning's lifelong conviction was that all adult men live in the consciousness of their incompleteness, yearing to become complete. Each of his speakers must accommodate these impulses, unsure often of what they signify. "O God, where do they tend—these struggling aims?" asks *Pauline's* poet. He answers his question with another: "And what is that I hunger for but God?" Paracelsus calls this restless spirit of anticipation "a tendency to God."

Browning found this tendency to God everywhere about him. He did not conceive of distinct processes of development for a natural

34. *Robert Browning and Julia Wedgwood*, pp. 54–55.

world and a human or spiritual world. In man's nature and in physical nature he perceived energy in motion, and he believed that it was directed. From his observations he deduced a first cause and an orderly process or law. However, he parted company with nineteenth-century evolutionists in finding not only a beginning to evolutionary process, but also an end toward which all creation was moving. God was in the beginning, is now, and will be in the future. In 1881, Browning carefully explained his understanding of evolutionary process to Dr. F. J. Furnivall, delineating both his agreements and his disagreement with naturalistic evolutionary theory:

> In reality, all that seems proved in Darwin's scheme was a conception familiar to me from the beginning: see in *Paracelsus* the progressive development from senseless matter to organized, until man's appearance (Part V). Also in *Cleon,* see the order of "life's mechanics,"—and I daresay in many passages of my poetry: for how can one look at Nature as a whole and doubt that, wherever there is a gap, a "link" must be "missing"—through the limited power and opportunity of the looker? But go back and back, as you please, *at* the back, as Mr. Sludge is made to insist, you find (*my* faith is as constant) creative intelligence, acting as matter but not resulting from it. Once set the balls rolling, and ball may hit ball and send any number in any direction over the table; but I believe in the cue pushed by a hand. When one is taunted (as I noticed is often fancied an easy method with the un-Darwinized)—taunted with thinking successive acts of creation credible, metaphysics have been stopped short, at, however physics may fare: time and space being purely conceptions of our own, wholly inapplicable to intelligence of another kind—with whom, as I made Luria say, there is an "everlasting moment of creation," if one at all,—past, present, and future, one and the same state. This consideration does not affect Darwinism proper in any degree. But I do not consider that his case as to the changes in organization, brought about by desire and will in the creature, proved. Tortoises never saw their own shells, top or bottom, nor those of their females, and are diversely variegated all over, each species after its own pattern.[35]

35. *Letters from Robert Browning to Various Correspondents,* first series, I, 83–85. In William Clyde DeVane Jr., *Browning's Parleyings: The Autobiography of a Mind,* p. 198.

Quite willing to agree with Darwin that evolutionary change has occurred, Browning refused to grant that selection among species has been natural rather than supernatural. Admitting that time and space are human conceptions, he would not force God to obey their laws. Rather than reduce natural and human phenomena to human categories alone, he would have man and nature strain forward to reach the God who awaits him at the end of time. Browning was interested in the origins of life, but he was vitally concerned about the ultimate of life. That ultimate, which he conceived of as being both above and ahead of nature, he called God. It was somewhat important to know whence man came, but of infinite importance to know where he was going. The emphasis of scientific evolution upon the physical origins of man could not account for man's moral consciousness and his spiritual yearnings. That men were somewhat like animals was undeniable; that they could become somewhat like God, a possibility which strict naturalism could not entertain, was equally obvious to Browning. Thwarted by its finitude, all creation everywhere seeks infinity.

The nature of the future which lures men onward remained nebulous for Browning. Santayana complained that Browning "had no idea of anything eternal; and so he gave, as he would probably have said, a filling to the empty Christian immortality by making every man busy in it about many things." This busyness consisted of "an infinite number of days to live through, an infinite number of dinners to eat, with an infinity of fresh fights and new love-affairs, and no end of last rides together."[36] There is nothing uniquely Christian about such an immortality. It is in fact simply an extension and improvement upon today's manifold activities. Prince Hohenstiel-Schwangau, for example, finds

> The Present an improvement on the Past,
> And promise for the Future—which shall prove
> Only the Present with its rough made smooth,
> Its indistinctness emphasized.
>
> [424–427]

The lyric *Reverie* also defines the future in terms of present actions:

---

36. "The Poetry of Barbarism," *Interpretations of Poetry and Religion*, 1900. Reprinted in *Robert Browning: A Collection of Critical Essays* edited by Philip Drew, p. 28.

Then life is—to wake not sleep,
   Rise and not rest, but press
From earth's level where blindly creep
   Things perfected, more or less,
To the heaven's height, far and steep,

Where, amid what strifes and storms
   May wait the adventurous quest,
Power is Love—transports, transforms
   Who aspired from worst to best,
Sought the soul's world, spurned the worms'.

                         [201–210]

Browning could not visualize an idle heaven, because he could not live an idle life. But the exact nature of life beyond death did not really concern him, any more than he bothered with metaphysical definitions of God. Heaven and God were unseen and unknown. More often than not, when Browning referred to immortality, Heaven and God were one in his thinking, as were hope and future.

Browning founded his arguments for personal immortality upon the same basis as his belief in God—human nature. Although, as has been noted, he observed progress in natural phenomena and believed in a supernaturally directed evolutionary process, he returned to human ontology for justifying his belief in heaven. Often considered the keenest psychologist of the Victorian writers, he could never be classified as a forerunner of twentieth-century psychoanalytic schools of psychology. Whereas Sigmund Freud and his followers sought the explanation for human behavior in instincts, in pleasure-oriented motives, or in drives for release from tensions, Browning as a psychologist takes his rightful place among post-Freudian psychologists like William Glasser or Gordon Allport, who insist that behavioral characterists cannot be interpreted adequately with reference primarily to the past. While not denying the value of the contributions of earlier psychological thought, Allport accepts man as unique and not simply as a more fully developed animal (behaviorism) or a determined, instinctive being (Freudianism). He stresses "propriate striving," among other human characteristics, the importance in motivation of "the possession of long-range goals" which distinguish "the human being from the animal, the adult from the child, and in many cases the healthy personality from the sick."[37] He would have psychol-

___

37. *Becoming: Basic Considerations for a Psychology of Personality*, p. 51.

ogy follow people's actual behavior, which is future-oriented, instead of tracing their past records. According to Allport,

> faith is basically man's belief in the validity and attainability of some goal (value). The goal is set by desires. Desires, however, are not merely pushes from behind (drive ridden). They include complex, future-oriented states as longing for a better world, for one's own perfection, for a completely satisfying relation to the universe. . . . It is this inseparability of the idea of the end from the course of the striving that we call faith.[38]

Allport's description of faith in the future is embodied in Browning's Abt Vogler, who hopes to find the "broken arcs" on earth transformed, in heaven, into "a perfect round":

> All we have willed or hoped or dreamed of good shall exist;
>   Not its semblance, but itself; no beauty, nor good, nor power
> Whose voice has gone forth, but each survives for the melodist
>   When eternity affirms the conception of an hour.
> The high that proved too high, the heroic for earth too hard,
>   The passion that left the ground to lose itself in the sky,
> Are music sent up to God by the lover and the bard;
>   Enough that he heard it once: we shall hear it by-and-by.
>   [Part X]

Gordon Allport's summary of his psychological interpretation of human behavior sounds strikingly similar to Browning's insistence upon choice of goals and commitment to them:

> To summarize: the most comprehensive units in personality are broad intentional dispositions, future-pointed. These characteristics are unique for each person, and tend to attract, guide, inhibit the more elementary units to accord with the major intentions themselves. This proposition is valid in spite of the large amount of unordered, impulsive, and conflictful behavior in every life. Finally, these cardinal characteristics are not infinite in number but for any given life in adult years are relatively few and ascertainable.[39]

38. *The Individual and His Religion*, p. 149.
39. *Becoming*, p. 92.

In reference to Browning, we would have to add only that the future never loses its attractive power, even at death. When earthly goals are no longer possible, the lure of immortality replaces them. Browning unvaryingly maintained that life implies growth, and growth implies future.

Recent theological studies have joined psychology in asserting the primacy of the future in man's experience. Substituting theological terms like *eschatology* and *apocalypse* for psychological ones like *propriate striving* and *goal-orientation,* theologians now insist that no man can live without eschatology. In the twentieth century, in spite of the increase of scientific technology, apocalyptic myths have flourished: Nazism, Fascism, Communism, and some radical forms of nationalism and racism. Each has had its own eschatology; each has pointed its adherents to a new age, eliciting new hope, organizing and disciplining followers. Every great social movement has flourished by appealing to inherent human desires to believe in a future. Contemporary civilization, though threatened by the possibility of atomic annihilation, has not quenched the human thirst for something to hope for, to believe in. In theological circles, religious thinkers have been able to answer the radical theologians who have proclaimed "God is dead" by simply pointing out that hope is not dead. Men continue to hope for a better tomorrow, and most men, these theologians believe, equate their hope in tomorrow with God. Wolfhart Pannenberg writes, for example, that "the message of the coming Kingdom of God implies that God in his very being is the future of the world"[40] Bishop Robinson contends that the meaning of hope is so similar to the meaning of God that it can stand for it. "At least it is a way in for those for whom the word *God* does not have much meaning any longer."[41] Both these men follow the reasoning of Paul Tillich:

> And if these words [*Kingdom of God* and *Divine Providence*] do not have much meaning for you, translate them, and speak of the depth of history, of the ground and aim of our social life, and of what you take seriously without reservation in your moral and political activities. Perhaps you should call this depth *hope,* simply hope. For if you find hope in the ground of history, you are united with the great prophets who were able to look into the depth of their times, who tried to escape it, because they could not stand the

40. *Theology and the Kingdom of God,* p. 61.
41. *In the End God,* p. 207.

horror of their visions, and who yet had the strength to look to an even deeper level and there to discover hope.[42]

The twentieth-century theological equations of hope with God state Browning's attitude toward the future more bluntly, but not less accurately, than he would have done. When he bids his readers "Greet the unseen with a cheer," the "unseen" ambiguously serves as a substantive for the place of the future and the Person in the future. Speaking at times of the God who controls the universe and rewards the just and the unjust, Browning nevertheless frequently speaks of the future, as he does in the "Epilogue" to *Asolando,* as a place of striving, speeding, and fighting quite like earth, in which the promised rewards of God seem to be forgotten. In his latest poems, God seems much less important than the future *per se,* "That all-including Future!"

> What were life
> Did soul stand still therein, forego her strife
> Through the ambiguous Present to the goal
> Of some all-reconciling Future? Soul,
> Nothing has been which shall not bettered be
> Hereafter,—leave the root, by law's decree
> Whence springs the ultimate and perfect tree!
>
> [367–373]

At times he sounds as if he trusts faith in the future more than he trusts the God of the future:

> Even as the world its life,
> So have I lived my own—
> Power seen with Love at strife,
> That sure, this dimly shown,
> —Good rare and evil rife.
>
> Whereof the effect be—faith
> That, some far day, were found
> Ripeness in things now rather,
> Wrong righted, each chain unbound,
> Renewal born out of scathe.

---

42. *The Shaking of the Foundations,* p. 59.

Why faith—but to lift the load,
    To leaven the lump, where lies
Mind prostrate through knowledge owed
    To the loveless Power it tries
To withstand, how vain!

[*Reverie*, 171–185]

The "tendency to God" which Browning mentioned in his early poems becomes in his last poems a faith in hope, an intense conviction that the struggles of life will not have been in vain. He must continue to press forward; when he ceases to believe in the future, he will die. It does not matter so much whether he speaks of God or of hope or of the future as it matters that he continues to look ahead. The tenuousness of existence, the prevalence of evil, the strain of righteousness require the assurance of an unseen tomorrow. In choosing to hope in spite of everything, Browning anticipates current theologians of hope, for whom Jürgen Moltmann speaks:

> Christian theology has one way in which it can prove its truth by reference to the reality of man and the reality of the world that concerns man—namely, by accepting the questionableness of human existence and the questionableness of human nature and the world which is disclosed by the event of promise. "Threatened by death" and "subjected to vanity"—that is the expression of our universal experience of existence and the world. "In hope"—that is manifestly the way in which Christian theology takes up these questions and directs them to the promised future of God.[43]

Moltmann's point is echoed by Harvey Cox, who believes that "given the empirical evidence around us," this kind of hope "can be held only in the most daring act of effrontery."[44] Cox refers to the hope which can look forward through "such totally unfunny challenges as war, death, and gratuitous suffering." Browning's hope is that which looks forward through man's ignorance, weakness, finitude, loneliness, and probationary trials to a future fulfillment for which there is no evidence, for a perfection for which he has no guarantee. His hope is not the serene acceptance of medieval man, whose world was ordered if not orderly. Nor does he share the nineteenth-century

43. *The Theology of Hope*, p. 94.
44. *The Feast of Fools*, p. 156.

liberal's anticipation that, thanks to industrial and scientific advances, progress toward a better life is inevitable. He certainly does not believe in the earthly perfectability of man or society. His is the hope of the last resort, the only alternative to despair. He hopes that human suffering and cruelty, physical and moral evil, and the mysteries of life do have meaning which will one day be revealed. Browning saw the same phenomena which depress the most thoroughgoing pessimist; he asked the same unanswerable questions of the universe. But in an act of faith he chose—irrationally and subjectively—to believe that his life was not in vain, that the tremendous urgings of nature do tend toward future reconciliation in God. He avoided both the sin of presumptions and the sin of despair. He did not adopt the attitude of the presumptuous Prometheus, stealing fire from the gods in order to make men like gods. He likewise refused the despairing attitude of Sisyphus, who struggles forever with no prospect of progress or fulfillment. He accepted the struggle, in his station below the gods, but chose to hope that fulfillment was forthcoming.

That Browning's hope derived from his sense of man's incompleteness and ignorance has already been stressed. What is remarkable about his attitude, however, is that he not only did not complain against his ignorance but indeed transformed it into a blessing. He expressed this strange attitude to Miss Barrett in 1846, when he wrote to her of the blessedness of love's necessary ignorance:

> What a divinely merciful thought of God for our sake . . . that we cannot *know* each other—infallibly know—as we know other things, in their qualities! For instance, I bid you know my love for you (which would be knowing *me*)—I complain that you do not, cannot—yet,—if you *could* . . . my Ba, would you have been ever quite my Ba? If you said, calmly as when judging of material objects, "there is affection, so much, and sincerity, and admiration & c., yes, *that* I see, of course, for it is *there,* plainly"—first of the fact, as *I* know it; and then of *this;* that you *desired* to know it, chose to lean forward, and take my poor testimony *for* a fact, believing through desire, or at least will to believe—so that I do, in the exercise of common sense, adore you, more and more, as I live to see more, and feel more.[45]

45. April 18, 1846. *The Letters of Robert Browning and Elizabeth Barrett Browning,* II, p. 86.

Incomplete knowledge of each other leads to more intense desire than full knowledge would elicit. Browning interpreted incomplete spiritual knowledge as the same kind of blessing. In answering Dr. Furnivall's questions on sections II and III of *Parleying with Bernard de Mandeville,* Browning again accepts human limitations, then converts them into a blessing:

> I should prosaically state the meaning thus: I do not ask a full disclosure of Truth, which would be a concession contrary to the law of things, which applies equally to the body and the soul, that it is only by striving to attain strength (in the one case) and truth (in the other) that body and soul do so—the effort (common to both) being productive, in each instance, of the necessary initiation into all the satisfactions which result from partial success; absolute success being only attainable for the body in full manhood—for the soul, in its full apprehension of Truth—which will be, not *here,* at all events.[46]

From incompleteness and ignorance arises hope. In all things physical or spiritual, hope is one of the bases of life. Browning believed what he had Paracelsus learn, that "hope and fear and love shall keep thee man!"

In 1877, Robert Browning wrote a poem which states explicitly the attitude toward the future which characterizes all his poetry from *Pauline* to *Asolando.* Written when the poet was still shaken by the abrupt death of his dear friend Ann Egerton-Smith, *La Saisiaz* expresses Browning's deepest emotions about life beyond the grave and his characteristic reasons for belief in immortality. He follows the precedent of *Bishop Blougram's Apology* in stripping his vocabulary of any Christian terms or presuppositions, and argues for immortality without recourse to revelation. In so doing, he employs arguments which in this study have become commonplace. Although the subject of the poem is immortality, this theme cannot be considered apart from Browning's other religious convictions: the existential nature of man, who subjects all facts and choices to personal judgment; the limitations of man, who escapes bondage to himself through projection into other personalities and times; the necessity of a future which calls man into himself, drawing him purposefully through his probatio-

---

46. March 2, 1889. *Letters of Robert Browning Collected by Thomas J. Wise,* edited by Thurman L. Hood, p. 301.

nary period into his fulfillment; and the reality of a God who informs and presides over all.

Browning's primary question in the poem is twofold: "Does the soul survive the body? Is there God's self, no or yes?" The quiet philosophical tone of the poem does not expose the agitation Browning felt when he asked these questions. Robert Buchanan met him during this period following Miss Egerton-Smith's death. He found the man whose words on death and immortality had inspired others completely distraught by this personal blow. The death of his friend was severe in itself; as a reminder of the earlier death of his wife, it was devastating. *La Saisiaz* is more than a literary elegy, therefore. It is Browning's personal confrontation with the earthly finality of death. In facing death he seeks the meaning of life, of God. He knows that he cannot find complete satisfaction for his quest, but he asks, nonetheless, confident that he can at least find as much truth as his human nature will allow:

> Well, and wherefore shall it daunt me, when 't is I
>   myself am tasked,
> When, by weakness weakness questioned, weakly answers—
>   weakly asked?
> Weakness never needs be falseness: truth is truth
>   in each degree
> —Thunderpealed by God to Nature, whispered by my soul
>   to me.
> Nay, the weakness turns to strength and triumphs in a
>   truth beyond:
> "Mine is but man's truest answer—how were it did God
>   respond?
>   [147–152]

His starting point is, as always, an affirmation of his own existence and, by implication, the existence of God:

> I have questioned and am answered. Question, answer
>   presuppose
> Two points: that the thing itself which questions,
>   answers,—*is*, it knows;
> As it also knows the thing perceived outside itself,
>   —a force

153

Actual ere its own beginning, operative through its course,
Unaffected by its end,—that this thing likewise needs
        must be;
Call this—God, then, call that—soul, and both—the
        only facts for me.
Prove them facts? that they o'erpass my power of proving,
        proves them such:
Fact it is I know I know not something which is fact
        as much.

                [217–224]

The heart of the poem consists of a dialogue between Fancy and Reason, in which Fancy proposes several secondary facts which can be inferred from the primary facts of faith in oneself and in God. Reason offers justifications for Fancy's propositions, corroborating them by demonstrating their pragmatic and psychological value. Fancy finds no certainty more plain

Than this mere surmise that after body dies soul lives
        again.
Two, the only facts acknowledged late, are now increased
        to three—
God is, and the soul is, and, as certain, after death
        shall be.

                [406–408]

Reason agrees, promising that "Life to come will be improvement on the life that's now." Then Fancy bolsters his argument for a future life by proposing that in this way judgment is cared for:

        Ordain that, whether rich or poor
Present life is judged in aught man counts advantage—
        be it hope,
Be it fear that brightens, blackens most or least
        his horoscope,—
He, by absolute compulsion such as made him live at all,
Go on living to the fated end of life whate'er befall.
What though, as on the earth he darkling grovels, man descry
        the sphere,
Next life's—call it, heaven or freedom, close above and
        crystal-clear?

He shall find—say, hell to punish who in aught curtails
        the term,
Fain would act the butterfly before he has played out
        the worm.
God, soul, earth, heaven, hell,—five facts now: what
        is to desiderate?

                                [456–465]

"Nothing!" Reason responds, promising that "Soon shall things be unperplexed / And the right and wrong, now tangled, lie unravelled in the next." We must note parenthetically that Browning worries as little about precise definitions of heaven in Fancy's argument as he does elsewhere about the meaning of *soul* or *God*. The reality, not the terminology, is Browning's concern. He refuses to make words ultimate.

Fancy moves on the the sixth fact:

Not so fast! still more concession! not alone do I
        declare
Life must needs be borne,—I also will that man become
        aware
Life has worth incalculable, every moment that he spends
So much gain or loss for that next life which on this
        life depends.
Good, done here, be there rewarded,—evil, worked here,
        there amerced!

                                [475–479]

These six facts, agrees Reason, begin with the affirmation that "God there is, and soul there is, / And soul's earthly life-allotment." It is only "by hypothesis" that he then argues that "soul is bound to pass probation, prove its powers, and exercise / Sense and thought on fact." Browning's consistent reliance upon imagination to convince one to believe in God is demonstrated in both the structure and the language of this dialogue. Fancy always speaks first, leading the discussion to ideas into which Reason is hesitant to venture. Reason is encumbered by values which demand logical consistency and empirical proof. For the ultimate questions of life, such consistency and proof are impossible. Thus the best Reason can do is to argue "by hypothesis." Nonetheless, though there is no absolute assurance, he can at least hope:

So, I hope—no more than hope, but hope—no less than hope,
          because
I can fathom, by no plumb-line sunk in life's apparent
          laws,
How I may in any instance fix where change should meetly
          fall
Nor involve, by one revisal, abrogation of them all.

                         [535–538]

Throughout the poem, Browning makes no attempt to prove anything about the nature of the future. What he demonstrates is the
necessity to man of future and of hope:

                    Hope, however scant,
Makes the actual life worth leading; take the hope
           therein away,
All we have to do is surely not endure another day.

                         [242–244]

The inequities of this world are acceptable only if they can be viewed
as aiding man during his probationary period on his way to a better
life:

I have lived, then, done and suffered, loved and hated,
              learnt and taught
This—there is no reconciling wisdom with a world
              distraught,
Goodness with triumphant evil, power with failure in
           the aim,
If—(to my own sense, remember! though none other feel
           the same!)
If you bar me from assuming earth to be a pupil's place
And life, time,—with all their chances, changes,—just
              probation-space,
Mine, for me.

                         [265–271]

Daring to speak for no one but himself, Browning candidly admits
life's evil, but finds it all acceptable if he can only believe in a second
life. Here, in summary, is his creed:

But, O world outspread beneath me! only for myself
        I speak,
Nowise dare to play the spokesman for my brothers
        strong and weak,
Full and empty, wise and foolish, good and bad, in every age,
Every clime, I turn my eyes from, as in one or other stage
Of a torture writhe they, Job-like couched on dung
        and crazed with blains
—Wherefore? whereto? ask, the whirlwind what the dread
        voice thence explains!
I shall "vindicate no way of God's to man," nor stand
        apart,
"Laugh, be candid!" while I watch it traversing the human
        heart.
Traversed heart must tell its story uncommented on: no less
Mine results in "Only grant a second life, I acquiesce
In this present life as failure, count misfortune's
        worst assaults
Triumph, not defeat, assured that loss so much the more
        exaults
Gain about to be.

                         [349–361]

In *La Saisiaz*, Browning presents an eschatological faith. Building upon the data of human experience and recorded religious history, he believes in promised future events for which present proof is impossible. Nonetheless, the believer acts as if fulfillment of the promises were inevitable. He awaits their eschatological verification. In so doing, he gives expression to man's inherent need to grow toward a future which promises greater possibilities than the present. Man's need to hope is as fundamental as his need for love. If he cannot live without love, neither can he live without hope.

With this eschatological faith, Browning adds hope to love (and, somewhat less importantly, power, intelligence, and goodness) as synonyms for God. Each of these attributes of God is a human quality projected upon ineffable divinity. Human hope becomes objectified as Future, in which hope becomes reality. Unlike the other attributes of divinity, hope is nowhere named by Browning, but its presence is always felt. From *Pauline's* poet's "yearning" after God and Paracelsus's "tendency to God" to Johannes Agricola's belief that "'tis to God I speed so fast," it is evident that Browning conceives of God objectively as both above and ahead of men, attracting them upward toward a greater realization of their potential and onward toward ever-retreating goals. Subjectively, he employs the word *God* frequently to refer to those inner urgings which compel men toward the future.

In the poems of Browning's last period, the efforts to name God which characterize the early poems have disappeared. "Mind" and "Love" and "Will" are gone. The total inefficacy of words to describe God has convinced Browning that all words are inadequate symbols. God is, but He is above knowledge. Man's faith must be built upon what he can know through experience. He can know love and hope. These, then, are the basis of his faith, his ultimate concern. In a God he chooses to call Love, he can relate to his universe, because he has experienced love. Toward a God he does not name but has experienced through hope, he can direct his life. An almighty and all-wise God who loves infinitely and rewards justly satisfies every human yearning for transcendent reality, allowing every man to hope that someday his weak and unfinished self will be strong and perfect. There is no proof that this hope will become reality—but a man must hope, if he would be a man. He may choose, Browning believes, to name the object of that hope, or even the hope itself, *God*.

Bibliography

Allport, Gordon W. *Becoming: Basic Considerations for a Psychology of Personality.* New Haven: Yale University Press, 1960.

_____ . *The Individual and His Religion.* New York: The Macmillan Company, 1967.

Altick, Richard D. "The Private Life of Robert Browning," *Yale Review,* XLI (December 1951), 247–262.

Altick, Richard Daniel, and James F. Loucks, II. *Browning's Roman Murder Story: A Reading of "The Ring and the Book."* Chicago and London: University of Chicago Press, 1968.

Altizer, Thomas, and William Hamilton. *Radical Theology and the Death of God.* Indianapolis: Bobbs-Merrill, 1966.

Barrett, William. *Irrational Man: A Study in Existential Philosophy.* New York: Doubleday Anchor Book, 1962.

Browning, Robert. *Browning to His American Friends: Letters Between the Brownings, the Storys and James Russell Lowell 1841–1890,* edited by Gertrude Reese Hudson. New York: Barnes and Noble, 1965.

_____ . *Dearest Isa: Robert Browning's Letters to Isabella Blagden,* edited by Edward C. McAleer. Austin: University of Texas Press, 1951.

_____ . "Essay on Shelley." In *The Four Ages of Poetry, Etc.,* edited by H. F. B. Brett-Smith. Oxford: Basil Blackwell, 1921.

_____ . *Learned Lady: Letters from Robert Browning to Mrs. Thomas FitzGerald, 1876–1889,* edited by Edward C. McAleer. Cambridge: Harvard University Press, 1966.

_____ . *The Letters of Robert Browning and Elizabeth Barrett Browning, 1845–1846,* edited by Robert Barrett Browning. 2 vols. London: Smith, Elder and Company, 1906.

159

Bibliography

———. *Letters of Robert Browning Collected by Thomas J. Wise,* edited, with an Introduction and Notes, by Thurman L. Hood. New Haven: Yale University Press, 1933.

———. *Letters of the Brownings to George Barrett,* edited by Paul Landis with the assistance of Ronald E. Freeman. Urbana: University of Illinois Press, 1958.

———. *New Letters of Robert Browning,* edited by William Clyde DeVane and Kenneth Leslie Knickerbocker. New Haven: Yale University Press, 1950.

———. *Robert Browning and Alfred Domett,* edited by Frederic G. Kenyon. London: Smith, Elder and Company, 1906.

———. *Robert Browning and Julia Wedgwood: A Broken Friendship as Revealed by Their Letters,* edited by Richard Curle. New York: Frederick A. Stokes Company, 1937.

———. *The Works of Robert Browning,* edited by F. G. Kenyon. 10 vols. London: Ernest Benn Ltd., 1912.

Buber, Martin. *I and Thou,* translated by Walter Kaufman. New York: Charles Scribner's Sons, 1970.

Buckley, Jerome Hamilton. *The Victorian Temper: A Study in Literary Culture.* New York: Vintage Books, 1951.

Bush, Douglas. *Mythology and the Romantic Tradition in English Poetry.* Cambridge: Harvard University Press, 1937.

Chapman, John J. "Robert Browning." In *The Browning Critics,* edited by Boyd Litzinger and E. L. Knickerbocker. Lexington: University of Kentucky Press, 1967, pp. 37–55.

Charlton, H. B. "Browning as Dramatist." *Bulletin of The John Rylands Library,* XXIII (1939), 33–67.

Chesterton, G. K. *Robert Browning.* New York: *Macmillan's Pocket Library,* 1951.

Clarke, Helen Archibald. *Browning and His Century.* New York: Doubleday, Page and Company, 1912.

Cox, Harvey. *The Feast of Fools.* Cambridge: Harvard University Press, 1969.

Crowell, Norton B. *The Convex Glass: The Mind of Robert Browning.* The University of New Mexico Press, 1968.

———. *The Triple Soul: Browning's Theory of Knowledge.* University of New Mexico Press, 1963.

DeVane, William Clyde, Jr. *A Browning Handbook,* 2nd edition. New York: Appleton-Century-Crofts, Inc., 1955.

———. *Browning's Parleyings: The Autobiography of a Mind.* New Haven: Yale University Press, 1927.

Bibliography

Drew Philip. "Henry Jones on Browning's Optimism." *Victorian Poetry,* II (1965), 29–41.

Drew, Philip, editor. *Robert Browning: A Collection of Critical Essays.* Boston: Houghton Mifflin Company, 1966.

Duckworth, F. R. G. *Browning: Background and Conflict.* New York: E. P. Dutton & Co., Inc., 1932.

Ellmann, Richard, and Charles Feidelson, Jr. *The Modern Tradition: Backgrounds of Modern Literature.* New York: Oxford University Press, 1965.

Evans, Maurice. *English Poetry in the Sixteenth Century.* 2nd edition. London: Hutchinson University Library, 1967.

Fairchild, Hoxie N. *Religious Trends in English Poetry.* 5 vols. New York: Columbia University Press, 1957.

Faverty, Frederic E. *The Victorian Poets: A Guide to Research.* 2nd edition. Cambridge: Harvard University Press, 1968.

Gilkey, Langdon. *Naming the Whirlwind: The Renewal of God-Language.* Indianapolis and New York: The Bobbs-Merrill Company, 1969.

Herford, C. H. *Robert Browning.* New York: Dodd, Mead and Company, 1905.

Holmes, Stewart W. "Browning: Semantic Stutterer." *PMLA,* LX (1945), 231–255.

_____ ."Browning's *Sordello* and Jung." *PMLA*, LVI (1941), 758-796.

Honan, Park. *Browning's Characters: A study in Poetic Technique.* New Haven: Yale University Press, 1961.

Inge, William Ralph. *Studies of English Mystics.* New York: E. P. Dutton and Company, 1906.

James, William. *Varieties of Religious Experience.* New York: Modern Library, 1902.

Johnson, E. D. H. *Alien Vision of Victorian Poetry: Sources of the Poetic Imagination in Tennyson, Browning, and Arnold.* Princeton, N.J.: Princeton University Press, 1952; Hamden, Conn.: The Shoe String Press, Inc., 1963.

Jones, Henry. *Browning as a Philosophical and Religious Teacher.* 2nd edition. Glasgow: James Maclehose and Sons, 1902.

Jones, Rufus M. "Mysticism in Robert Browning." *The Biblical Review,* VIII (April 1923), 229–245.

Jones, W. T. *A History of Western Philosophy: Kant to Wittgenstein and Sartre.* New York: Harcourt, Brace and World, 1969.

Kenmare, Dallas. *An End to Darkness: A New Approach to Robert Browning and His Work.* London: Peter Owen Ltd., 1962.

161

Bibliography

Kierkegaard, Sören. *Fear and Trembling and The Sickness unto Death,* translated by Walter Lowrie. New York: Doubleday Anchor Book, 1954.

King, Roma A., Jr. *The Focusing Artifice: The Poetry of Robert Browning.* Athens, Ohio: Ohio University Press, 1968.

Langbaum, Robert. "Browning and the Question of Myth." *PMLA,* LXXXI (1966), 575–584.

——————. *The Poetry of Experience: The Dramatic Monologue in Modern Literary Tradition.* London: Chatto and Windus, 1957.

Litzinger, Boyd. *Time's Revenges: Browning's Reputation as a Thinker 1889–1962.* Knoxville: University of Tennessee Press, 1964.

Litzinger, Boyd, and K. L. Knickerbocker, editors. *The Browning Critics.* Lexington: University of Kentucky Press, 1967.

Loth, David. *The Brownings: A Victorian Idyll.* New York: Brentano's, 1929.

Miller, Betty. *Robert Browning.* London: John Murray, 1952.

Miller, J. Hillis. *The Disappearance of God.* New York: Schocken Books, 1965.

Moltmann, Jürgen. *The Theology of Hope.* New York and Evanston: Harper and Row, 1967.

Orr, Mrs. Sutherland. *Life and Letters of Robert Browning.* Boston and New York: Houghton Miffllin and Company, 1891.

Pannenberg, Wolfhart. *Theology and the Kingdom of God.* Philadelphia: The Westminster Press, 1969.

Raymond, William Ober. *The Infinite Moment and Other Essays on Robert Browning,* 2nd edition. Toronto: University of Toronto Press, 1965.

Renan, Ernst. *The Life of Jesus.* New York: Modern Library, 1955.

Robertson, John M. *Browning and Tennyson as Teachers.* London: A. and H. B. Bonner, 1903.

Robinson, John A. T. *In the End God.* New York: Harper and Row, 1968.

Santayana, George. "The Poetry of Barbarism." In *Interpretations of Poetry and Religion.* New York: Charles Scribner's Sons, 1900.

Schleiermacher, Friedrich. *On Religion: Address in Response to Its Cultured Critics,* translated by Terence N. Tice. Richmond: John Knox Press, 1969.

Sharp, William. *Life of Robert Browning.* London: Walter Scott, Ltd., 1897.

Shaw, David. *The Dialectical Temper: The Rhetorical Art of Robert Browning.* Ithaca: Cornell University Press, 1968.

Strauss, David Friedrich. *The Life of Jesus Critically Examined,* translated by George Eliot. New York: MacMillan and Company, 1892.

Bibliography

Teilhard de Chardin, Pierre. *How I Believe*. New York: Harper and Row, 1969.

Tillich, Paul. *Dynamics of Faith*. New York: Harper and Brothers Publishers, 1958.

_____ . *Love, Power and Justice*. New York: Oxford University Press, 1960.

_____ . *The Shaking of the Foundations*. New York: Charles Scribner's Sons, 1948.

Ward, Maisie. *Robert Browning and His World: The Private Face, 1812–1861*. New York: Holt, Rinehart and Winston, 1967.

_____ . *Robert Browning and His World: Two Robert Brownings? 1861–1889*. New York: Holt, Rinehart and Winston, 1969.

Wingfield-Stratford, Esmé. *Those Earnest Victorians*. William Morrow and Company, 1930.

Index

Index

Teilhard de Chardin, Pierre, 103-104
Tertullian, 24
Theology: Continental, 15; Death-of-God, 14, 148; liberalism, 16, 20-21; theology of hope, 21-22, 148; natural 95, 98, 99
Tillich, Paul, xi, 21, 24, 76, 93, 94, 96-97, 138, 148-149

Unamuno, Miguel, 24

Victorian England, 6, 14, 15

Ward, Maisie, 28, 29
Warren Commission, 120
Wedgwood, Julia, 58, 130, 131, 142-143
Whitman, Walter, 9
Wingfield-Stratford, Esmé, 91-92
Wiseman, Nicholas Patrick Stephen, 88
Wordsworth, William, 142